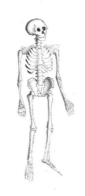

FASCINATING FACTS

KINGFISHER

NEW YORK

Contents

KINGFISHER
Larousse Kingfisher Chambers Inc.
95 Madison Avenue
New York, New York 10016

First published in 1999
The material in this edition was previously published
in four individual volumes in 1992.
10 9 8 7 6 5 4 3 2 1
1TR/0699/WKT/(FR)/115MA.

ISBN 0-7534-5265-0

LIBRARY OF CONGRESS CATALOGING-IN-PUBLICATION DATA
has been applied for.

Produced by Times Four Publishing Ltd.
Designed by Brian Robertson, Margaret Howdle, Chris
Leishman, Iain Ashman
Cover design by Terry Woodley
Additional text contributions by Catriona Macgregor
Consultant: Jill A. Wright
Illustrated by Peter Bull, Shelagh McNicholas, Guy Smith,
Michael Stewart, Sandra Hill, Ruth Lindsay

Printed in China

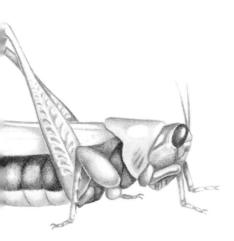

Introduction

In this book you will find over a thousand fascinating facts about the world around you. It will also give you remarkable insights into our amazing plant, the Earth, and the people who inhabit it. You can read about the rich and varied animal kingdom and discover the most incredible facts about space.

Also, there are lots of easy-to-find facts beginning with a spot, like this:

• By the time they are two years old, most children can use several hundred words.

Across the top of each page there is a list of useful **mini-facts**—for example, what the human body is made of, the world's rarest rain forest animals, the distance of the planets from the Sun, or the names of the earliest creatures on Earth.

On each double-page spread there is a **Strange but True** box containing especially unusual or startling facts.

If you are not sure where to find facts about a particular topic, look in the **Index** on pages 94–96.

To help you pick out the things you want to read about, some of the key words are in bold type like this: **Olympic Games**.

The Earth from Birth

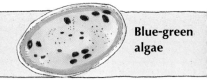

Blue-green algae

The Solar System was formed about **4.5 billion years** ago from a huge spinning cloud of gas and dust. The Sun was born at the center of the cloud.

Farther out, dust particles began to collect together as small lumps, which grew larger and larger as they collided. Eventually these became the **planets**, including the **Earth**.

The Earth started as a mass of red-hot rock. Around a billion years after it had formed, it was cool enough for oceans to form on the surface. These are where the first life forms developed.

Strange but true

- Fossilized footprints of early humans have been discovered in rocks.

- The biggest dinosaur was Seismosaurus. It weighed as much as 15 elephants.

- People once thought that fossils were the remains of dragons and giants.

- The Stegosaurus was 30 ft. (9 m) long, but had a brain the size of a walnut.

Earth's beginnings

The development of the Earth is divided into five lengths of time called **eras**. The first two eras, the **Archaean** and the **Proterozoic**, lasted for four billion years, which is almost **80 percent** of the Earth's history.

- During the Archaean Era, the Earth was born. Water and gases such as oxygen were formed. Very simple life forms appeared between 3.5 and 4 billion years ago.

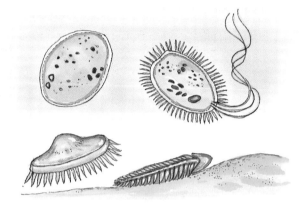

- During the Proterozoic Era, from about 2.5 billion to 570 million years ago, the first animals appeared in the sea. They were simple animals without backbones, such as worms and jellyfish.

- The Paleozoic era lasted from about 570 million years ago to 245 million years ago. During this time the Earth was covered in swamps. Larger plants, fish, and amphibians appeared.

- The Mesozoic era lasted from about 245 million years ago to 65 million years ago. In this period many animals developed, including giant reptiles called dinosaurs. The first mammals and birds also appeared.

- The Cenozoic era began about 65 million years ago and is still going on. The plants and animals we know today developed during this time.

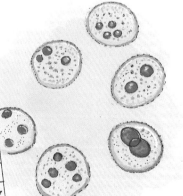

Microscopic plants called algae were among the first life forms.

How life began

When the Earth was young, a mixture of different chemicals covered its surface. The Sun's radiation acted on the chemicals and they formed new materials called **amino acids** and **sugars**.

The amino acids and sugars linked up and eventually living **cells** were created. Cells are the smallest units of life, from which all living things are made.

Fossils

Scientists can tell what early plants and animals were like by looking at **fossils**. A fossil is the hardened remains or shape of an animal or plant preserved in rock.

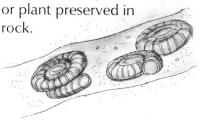

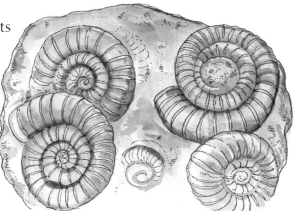

- A fossil forms when a dead animal or plant gets covered in mud or clay.

- The soft parts of the body decay, leaving the hard parts such as shell.

- Over thousands of years, the mud hardens into rock.

- Some animal and plant fossils have been found in pieces of amber, a fossilized resin which oozed from pine trees millions of years ago and then hardened.

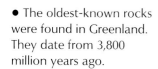 Fossil in amber

Greenland

- The oldest-known rocks were found in Greenland. They date from 3,800 million years ago.

Evolution

Evolution is the theory that animals and plants have gradually changed shape and form over millions of years, to enable them to survive in their surroundings. For instance, human beings probably evolved from apes.

Dinosaurs

Dinosaurs were the biggest land animals that ever lived. They were reptiles with scaly skins.

- Plant-eating dinosaurs were huge. Brachiosaurus and Diplodocus were some of the biggest, up to 100 ft. (30 m) in length.

- Meat-eating dinosaurs were smaller and ran on hind legs. The largest was Tyrannosaurus, which stood about 16 ft. (5 m) tall.

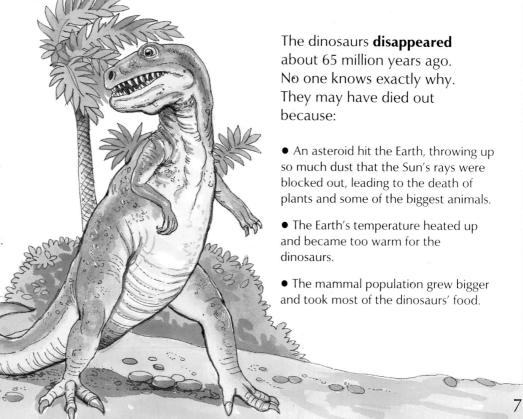

The dinosaurs **disappeared** about 65 million years ago. No one knows exactly why. They may have died out because:

- An asteroid hit the Earth, throwing up so much dust that the Sun's rays were blocked out, leading to the death of plants and some of the biggest animals.

- The Earth's temperature heated up and became too warm for the dinosaurs.

- The mammal population grew bigger and took most of the dinosaurs' food.

The Earth's Surface

Here are the seven continents:

Australia
3 million sq. miles
(7.7 million sq. km)

Asia
17 million
sq. miles
(44 million sq.

The Earth's outer shell is called the **crust**. It is divided into pieces called **plates**, which fit together rather like a jigsaw puzzle. They "float" on top of hot, partly molten rock (the **mantle**).

The crust forms the land and the ocean floor.

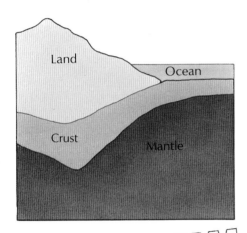

Land
Ocean
Crust
Mantle

The Earth's plates

The Earth's **plates** move around very, very slowly as they "float" on top of hot rock. As they move, they carry the land and the ocean floor with them. Sometimes the plates:

- Collide, pushing up mountains or creating deep ocean trenches and volcanoes (see p.12 and p.21).

- Slide slowly past each other, producing so much strain that they cause earthquakes (see p.14).

- Move apart so the ocean floor splits between them and molten rock rises up through cracks.

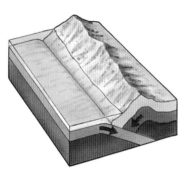

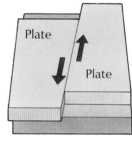

Plate

Plate

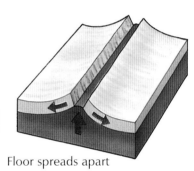

Floor spreads apart

Earth facts

- Greenland is the largest island in the world. It may possibly be several islands covered by a sheet of ice.

Greenland

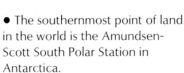

- The northernmost point of land in the world is the islet of Oodaq near the North Pole. It is covered in ice.

- The southernmost point of land in the world is the Amundsen-Scott South Polar Station in Antarctica.

- The highest point of land in the world is Mount Everest in the Himalayan mountain range.

Strange but true

- In the past, people thought that the oceans and continents were a result of Noah's flood.

- On average, the Earth's plates move between $\frac{1}{2}$ inch (1.3 cm) and 4 inches (10 cm) a year.

- The Atlantic Ocean is getting wider, but the Pacific Ocean is shrinking.

- Pangaea comes from an ancient Greek word meaning "whole Earth."

The continents

On maps, the land is divided into seven parts called **continents**. The continents are themselves moving, but very, very slowly — it has taken millions of years for them to reach where they are today.

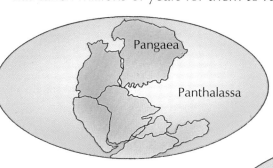

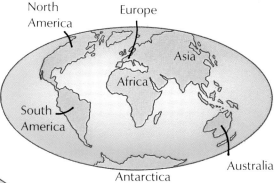

- About 120 million years ago there were two continents: Laurasia and Gondwanaland.

- Laurasia broke into North America, Europe, and Asia.

- The continents began as one big mass of land called Pangaea. It started to break up about 200 million years ago.

- Pangaea was surrounded by a single vast ocean called Panthalassa.

- Gondwanaland broke up to become Africa, South America, Antarctica, Australia, and India.

- The continents are still moving. For instance, North America moves away from Europe at a rate of about an inch (3 cm) a year.

The past and the future

Here are some examples of the shape of continents in the **past**:

- The east coast of South America and the west coast of Africa were joined.

- The continents of Africa and Antarctica were also joined. There is proof of this because fossilized remains of tropical African plants and animals have been found in modern Antarctica.

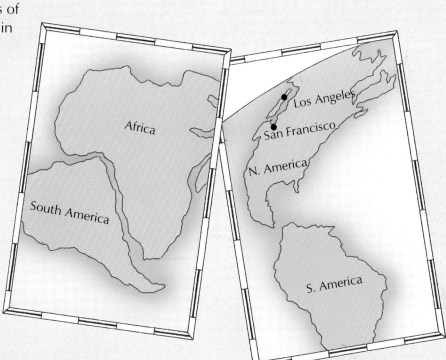

Here are some examples of what may occur in **50 million years** time:

- The two American continents will have broken apart.

- Africa and Asia will have broken apart.

- Part of California, including the city of Los Angeles, will have broken off from America.

Inside the Earth

Here are the four most precious gems to be found on the Earth:

Ruby

The Earth is made up of four layers. The thin outer layer is called the **crust**. Then comes the hot, partly molten rock of the **mantle**.

Beneath the mantle there is a layer of liquid metal called the **outer core**.

In the center of the Earth, there is a ball of very hot solid metal called the **inner core**.

Crust
Mantle
Outer core
Inner core

The Earth's layers

Scientists have worked out what is likely to be inside the Earth by analyzing **rocks** and by studying the **shock waves** that travel up to the surface during earthquakes (see pp.14–15).

- The Earth gets hotter toward its center. The temperature in the middle is thought to be more than 9,000°F (5,000°C).

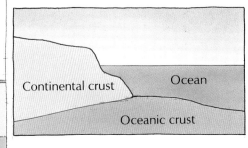

Continental crust
Ocean
Oceanic crust

- The deepest rock samples ever gathered came from a hole drilled 60 miles (100 km) down from the surface.

- New crust is being made all the time, as molten rock bubbles up through huge cracks between plates in the ocean floor. (see p.12).

- There are two kinds of Earth crust — ocean crust beneath the seas and continental crust beneath the land.

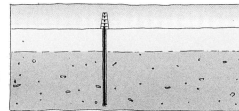

Strange but true

- Diamonds are harder than any other natural substance.

- Children playing on a beach made the first discovery of a South African diamond.

- The largest diamond ever found weighed over a pound (half a kilogram).

- Diamonds are made of the same substances as coal soot and other carbons.

Rocks

There are three different types of rock on Earth. They are given the names **igneous**, **sedimentary**, and **metamorphic**.

- Igneous rocks are formed when hot molten material called magma bubbles up from beneath the crust and hardens.

- Metamorphic rocks are rocks that have been changed and hardened by heat and pressure. Limestone, for example, can change into marble.

- Some sedimentary rocks are made from pieces of older rocks which collect in layers, usually beneath the sea. As the layers pile up, the material is squeezed into rock — sand becomes sandstone, mud becomes clay.

- Other sedimentary rocks form from layers of dead animals and plants on the seabed.

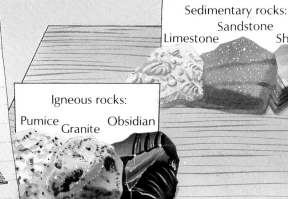

Sedimentary rocks:
Sandstone
Limestone   Shale

Igneous rocks:
Pumice   Obsidian
Granite

Metamorphic rocks:
Marble   Slate

10

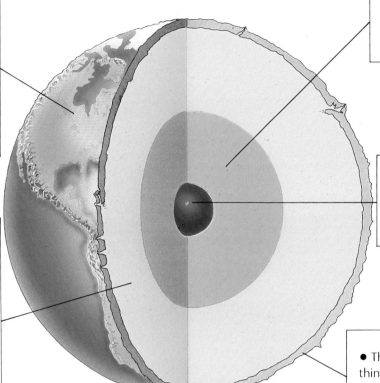

● The Earth's crust varies in thickness from 24.8 miles (40 km) beneath parts of the continents to only 3.1 miles (5 km) under parts of the ocean floor. It is made of lighter rock than the other layers. The temperature of the rocks increases by about 86°F (30°C) for every kilometer under the surface.

● The outer core is about 1,200 miles (2,000 km) thick. It is a mixture of very hot liquid iron and nickel.

● The inner core of the planet is thought to be a solid ball of iron and nickel that measures about 1,500 miles (2,400 km) across.

● The Earth's mantle is about 1,800 miles (2,900 km) thick. At the top it is made of solid rock. Deeper down it is so hot that the rock melts and becomes molten. The rock in the mantle layer is composed mainly of iron and magnesium.
　There is a definite boundary line between the crust and the mantle.

● The Earth's crust is only a very thin layer. Its upper surface is constantly being altered by weather and land movement.

Riches from the Earth

Our main sources of **heat and power** come from beneath the Earth's surface. Oil, gas, and coal are called **fossil fuels**.

● Oil is made from the bodies of tiny sea creatures that lived millions of years ago. The bodies gathered on the seabed and they were gradually squeezed down under rocks that formed above them. Eventually they turned into oil.

● Coal is made from trees that died millions of years ago. Layers of the dead plant material were squeezed down until they turned into carbon.

● Natural gas is made when animal and plant bodies decompose. It is usually found in the same place as oil.

Ocean oil platform

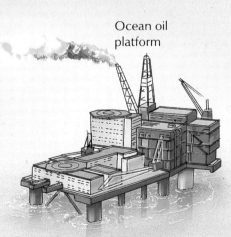

Gemstones

Precious stones are mined from beneath the Earth's surface.

● Gems form as crystals in igneous rock. They vary in color, shape, and size. Because they are rare, they have been prized for centuries.

● The rarest diamonds are blue or pink. Rubies are the rarest gems of all. The finest ones come from Myanmar (Burma).

● The best sapphires come from Myanmar (Burma), Kashmir, India, and Montana.

● The finest emeralds come from Colombia in South America.

11

Volcanoes and Geysers

Toothpaste

Volcanoes occur where hot liquid rock reaches the surface through cracks in the Earth's crust. Most volcanoes are found where two **plates** are pushing against one another or moving apart (see p.8).

Volcanoes that erupt are called active. Many of them are found in an area around the Pacific Ocean called the "**Pacific Ring Of Fire**."

Volcanoes in the Pacific Ring of Fire

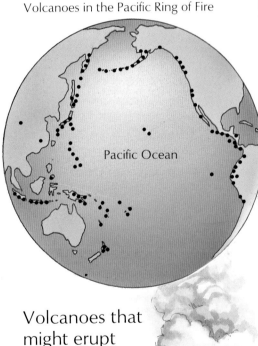

Pacific Ocean

Volcanoes that might erupt are **dormant**. Volcanoes that have stopped erupting are **extinct**.

This volcano is active.

How a volcano forms

Pressure builds up underground and pushes molten liquid rock up from a chamber beneath the surface. It spews out of a crack in the ground as **lava**.

Crater

Secondary cone

Layers of ash and lava

- Ash, lava, and rock build up to form a hill or mountain with a crater in the top. Sometimes, further eruptions of lava flow out of a secondary cone.

- Gas, lava, and pieces of solid rock (called tephra) spew out. Large molten lumps of tephra are called volcanic bombs.

Magma chamber

Hot springs and geysers

Hot springs occur when underground water is heated up by hot rocks beneath the Earth's surface. The boiling water rises up through cracks in the ground.

Geysers are hot springs of water heated up under pressure. Many spout water and steam at regular intervals.

- Yellowstone Park in Wyoming has over 2,500 geysers, including a world-famous one nicknamed "Old Faithful."

- New Zealand and Iceland are the other main areas of geyser activity.

- A fumarole is a crack in the ground that releases more gas than water. These often occur on volcano slopes.

A fumarole

Makeup

Bathtub cleaner

Road surfacing material

Volcano shapes

A **volcano's shape** depends on the type of eruption that caused it and the sort of material that comes out.

- Shield volcanoes are shaped like upturned saucers, with gentle slopes.

- Cinder cone volcanoes are high, with steep slopes.

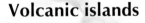

- Strata-volcanoes are cone-shaped mountains.

Types of eruption

Eruptions are given different names, depending on how strong they are.

- Hawaiian eruptions are not very violent. They pour out liquid lava in fiery rivers.

- Strombolian eruptions pour out thicker lava, but not very violently. Strombolian volcanoes erupt continuously.

- Vulcanian eruptions produce violent explosions and throw out tephra, dust, gas, and ash.

- Peléean eruptions are gigantic explosions which throw out a huge cloud of gas and lava.

Strange but true

- In 1783 an Icelandic eruption threw up enough dust to temporarily block out the Sun over Europe.

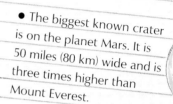

- The biggest known crater is on the planet Mars. It is 50 miles (80 km) wide and is three times higher than Mount Everest.

- Hot water from geysers is used to heat homes and offices in Reykjavic, capital of Iceland.

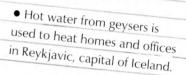

- About 20 to 30 volcanoes erupt each year, mostly under the sea.

Volcanic islands

Many **ocean islands** have been formed by volcanic eruptions beneath the sea. First ash is blown above the water and then a pile of rock and lava builds up until it appears above the waves.

- In 1963 the volcanic island of Surtsey appeared near Iceland. It took three weeks to rise from the waves.

- In 1883 the volcanic island of Krakatoa, near Java, blew up. Rock blasted 50 miles (80 km) into the air.

Pompeii

In A.D. 79 the Italian volcano **Vesuvius** erupted and buried the Roman cities of **Pompeii** and **Herculaneum**.

- The cities were hidden for nearly seventeen centuries, until a farmer discovered some ruins in 1748.

- Vesuvius is still an active volcano. If it erupted in the future, the nearby city of Naples would have to be evacuated.

Earthquakes

Pigeons

Earthquakes are severe shocks that happen when powerful **vibrations** pass from underground up to the surface through solid rock. The ground shakes violently and huge cracks may appear. Some are wide enough to swallow cars.

Earthquakes happen where two of the Earth's **plates** meet. The pressure of the plates pushing against each other causes deep cracks in the rock called **fault lines**.

The rocks on either side of a fault line sometimes slide up or along. This makes them bend and shatter, causing earthquake **shock waves**.

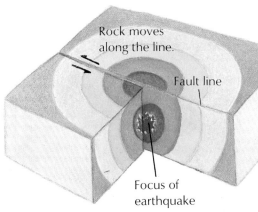

Rock moves along the line.

Fault line

Focus of earthquake

Earthquake profile

An earthquake begins beneath the ground at the point where the rocks move.

- The point where the earthquake begins underground is called the focus.

- The point on the surface above the focus is called the epicenter.

The movement creates **waves of energy** which travel up to the surface.

Epicenter on the surface

Shock waves

Focus underground

- There may be lots more minor earthquakes called aftershocks after the first earthquake. These occur because the rocks beneath are falling back into place.

Earthquake areas

- Most earthquakes happen around the edges of the Pacific Ocean or near mountainous areas such as the Himalayas.

- The San Andreas Fault runs through California. In 1906, the rocks on one side of the fault moved 15 ft. (4.6 meters), causing an earthquake.

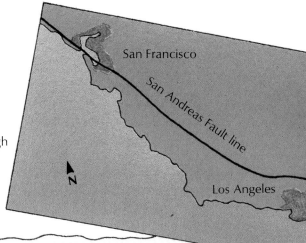

San Francisco

San Andreas Fault line

N

Los Angeles

Earthquake buildings

- Earthquake-proof buildings are built with reinforced steel or concrete frames on a solid platform. Many skyscrapers in San Francisco are built this way.

Earthquake effects

An earthquake can cause:

- A series of gigantic fast-moving waves called tsunami. The biggest one ever seen was 220 ft. (67 m) tall, the height of about 9 houses!

- Dangerous mud and rock avalanches that engulf the surrounding land.

- Fires set off by broken gas pipes and electrical cables.

Measuring earthquakes

Earthquakes are measured using the **Richter Scale** or the **Mercalli Scale**. The Richter Scale has 8 numbers that measure earthquake energy. Each number denotes 10 times more energy than the number before. The Mercalli Scale has 12 numbers measuring the effect of an earthquake on objects and buildings.

Examples of Richter numbers:

1·2	5	7	8
Barely noticeable	Some damage	Like a nuclear bomb	Total devastation

Examples of Mercalli numbers

II	V	VII	XII
Lamps swing and windows shake	Dishes smash	Walls collapse	Total damage

Predicting earthquakes

Scientists monitor earthquake areas to predict tremors. There are **monitoring stations** all over the world that measure Earth movement. Some early signs of earthquakes are shown below:

• A radioactive gas called radon is released from rocks. Scientists monitor well water to detect increases in radon traces.

• Small tremors called foreshocks happen just before an earthquake. The ground swells up and cracks.

• Animals behave oddly. They are often very sensitive to tremors.

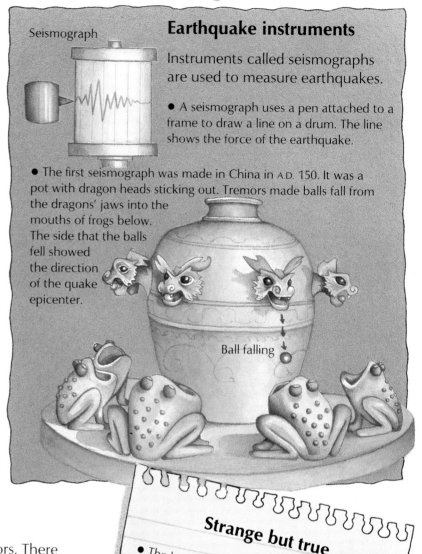

Earthquake instruments

Seismograph

Instruments called seismographs are used to measure earthquakes.

• A seismograph uses a pen attached to a frame to draw a line on a drum. The line shows the force of the earthquake.

• The first seismograph was made in China in A.D. 150. It was a pot with dragon heads sticking out. Tremors made balls fall from the dragons' jaws into the mouths of frogs below. The side that the balls fell showed the direction of the quake epicenter.

Ball falling

Strange but true

• The longest earthquake known lasted for 38 days.

• There are thousands of earthquakes a year. Only 20 to 30 are felt by people.

• In 1975 the Chinese city of Haicheng was evacuated 2 hours before an earthquake because people noticed their animals behaving oddly.

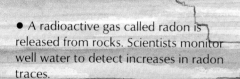

Mountains and Valleys

Here are the highest land mountains in order of height:

Mt. Everest Himalayas 29,028 ft. (8,848 m)

ountains are rock masses that are at least 2,000 ft. (600 m.) high. They are usually found in groups called **ranges** or **chains**. They cover about one quarter of the Earth's land surface.

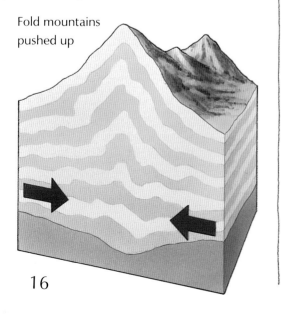

A mountain range

Most of the world's tallest mountain ranges were built when two of the Earth's **plates** collided with each other, slowly pushing up the rock above. Mountain building takes millions of years. It is still going on today.

Fold mountains pushed up

Types of mountain

There are four different types of mountain, called **fold**, **block**, **volcanic**, and **dome**.

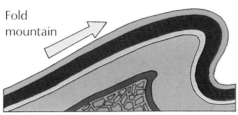

Fold mountain

Block mountain

● Fold mountains occur when two of the Earth's plates push against each other. The rock in the middle is pushed up in folds.

● Sometimes two faults (deep rock cracks) run alongside each other. Pressure heaves up the block of land in the middle.

● A volcanic mountain grows when lava, dust, and ashes gradually build up in a cone shape (see pp.12–13).

● Dome mountains are created when hot volcanic material rises upward from deep in the Earth and pushes the rocks above into a dome shape.

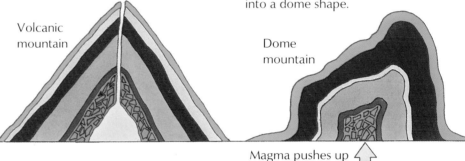

Volcanic mountain

Dome mountain

Magma pushes up

Mountain areas

There are **mountain ranges** all over the world. The largest ones are shown on the map below.

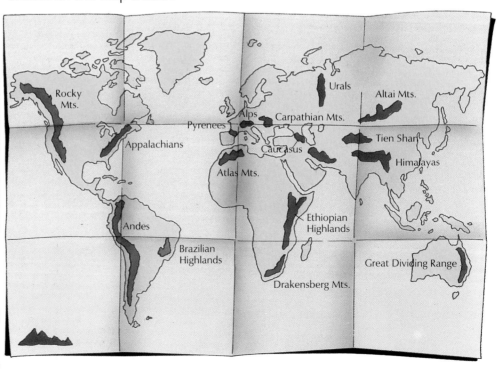

Rocky Mts.
Urals
Altai Mts.
Alps
Carpathian Mts.
Pyrenees
Appalachians
Tien Shan
Caucasus
Himalayas
Atlas Mts.
Andes
Ethiopian Highlands
Brazilian Highlands
Drakensberg Mts.
Great Dividing Range

K2
Himalayas
28,250 ft.
(8,611 m)

Kanchenjunga
Himalayas 28,208 ft.
(8,598 m.)

Makalu
Himalayas 27,824 ft.
(8,481 m.)

Dhaulagiri
Himalayas
26,793 ft.
(8,167 m.)

Mountain profile

At the bottom of a mountain there may be a forest of **deciduous trees**, which lose their leaves in winter. In hot, wet areas, there may be **rain forest**.

Further up, there are likely to be **coniferous trees**. Most of these stay green all year round.

The place where the trees stop growing is called the **tree line**. Above this line only hardy alpine plants, grasses, and mosses grow.

Finally, the temperature gets too cold for plants to grow. On the top of high mountains it is so cold that there is snow all year round. Below this the snow will melt in summer. The line between the two areas is called the **snow line**.

Snow stays all year round

Snow line

This snow melts in summer

Alpine plants, grasses, and mosses

Coniferous fir trees

Deciduous trees (rain forest in hot, wet areas)

Strange but true

• The Andes and the Himalayas are still rising, but their rocks are being worn away.

• The lowest officially-named hill stands 15 ft. (4.5 m.) high on a golf course in Brunei.

• Mount Everest is 20 times higher than the world's tallest building, the Sears Tower in Chicago.

Glaciers and valleys

A **glacier** is a huge mass of ice that moves down a valley under its own weight. A glacier:

• Moves along very slowly.

• Carves out a U-shaped valley as it travels along.

When winter snow melts on a mountainside, the water flows into **rivers**. A river:

• Carves out a V-shaped valley as it travels.

• May carve a steep-sided valley called a gorge.

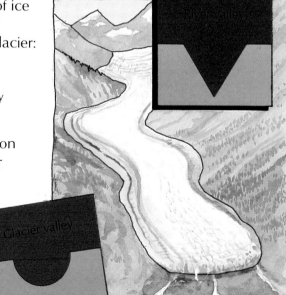

River valley

Glacier valley

17

Rivers and Lakes

Nile
Africa
4,145 miles (6,670 km)

Rivers begin on higher land and flow downhill to the sea. They may start from **underground springs**, or from melting **snow** or **glaciers**.

A river's route is divided into three parts. The first part is called the **upper course**, where the river flows steeply downhill and the current is fast. The water carries sand, gravel, and rocks down with it.

Upper course

Middle course

Lower course

In the **middle course** the river flows along a gentler slope. It travels more slowly but it still wears away rock and sand from its banks.

In the **lower course** the river slows down and gets wider. Some of the sand and rock it has been carrying is now worn down into tiny particles called **silt**.

River profile

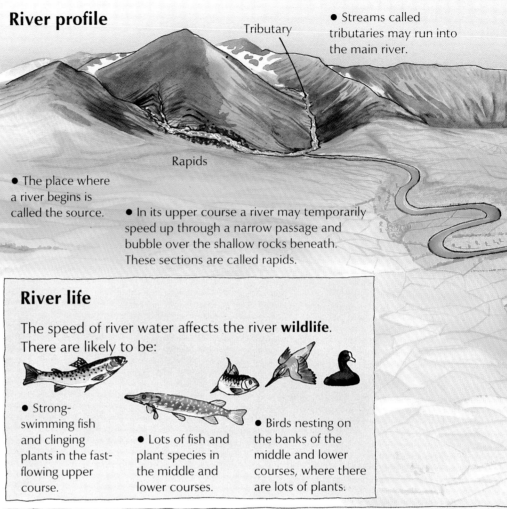

Tributary

● Streams called tributaries may run into the main river.

Rapids

● The place where a river begins is called the source.

● In its upper course a river may temporarily speed up through a narrow passage and bubble over the shallow rocks beneath. These sections are called rapids.

River life

The speed of river water affects the river **wildlife**. There are likely to be:

● Strong-swimming fish and clinging plants in the fast-flowing upper course.

● Lots of fish and plant species in the middle and lower courses.

● Birds nesting on the banks of the middle and lower courses, where there are lots of plants.

Lakes

A **lake** is an area of water surrounded by land. Lakes occur where water can collect in hollows in the ground, or behind natural or artificial barriers. Lakes can be:

● Very large. The world's biggest freshwater lake is Lake Superior in the U.S. and Canada. It covers a vast area of over 31,777 sq. miles (82,300 sq. km.)

● Very deep. The world's deepest lake is Lake Baykal in Russia. Its deepest crevice goes down 6,365 ft. (1,940 m).

 **Amazon**
S. America 4,007 miles
(6,448 km)

 Yangtze
Asia 3,915 miles
(6,300 km)

 Mississippi-Missouri
N. America
3,741 miles (6,020 km)

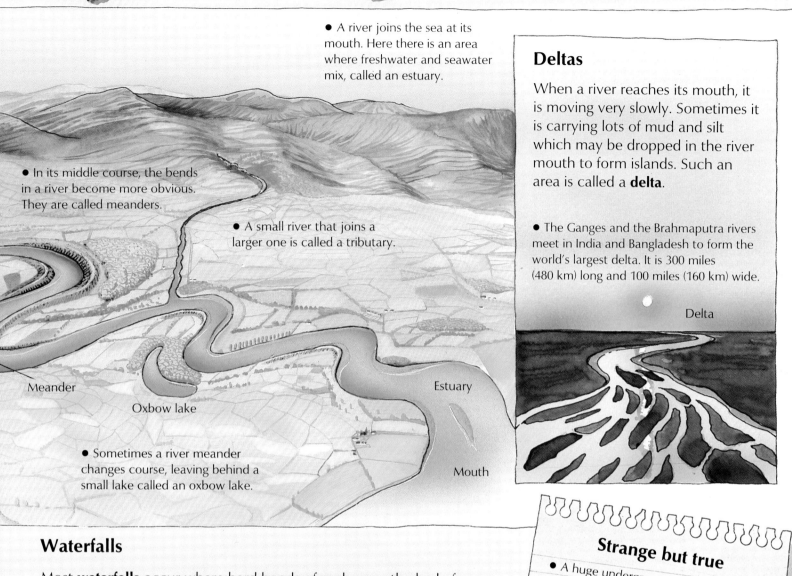

● A river joins the sea at its mouth. Here there is an area where freshwater and seawater mix, called an estuary.

● In its middle course, the bends in a river become more obvious. They are called meanders.

● A small river that joins a larger one is called a tributary.

Meander

Oxbow lake

● Sometimes a river meander changes course, leaving behind a small lake called an oxbow lake.

Estuary

Mouth

Deltas

When a river reaches its mouth, it is moving very slowly. Sometimes it is carrying lots of mud and silt which may be dropped in the river mouth to form islands. Such an area is called a **delta**.

● The Ganges and the Brahmaputra rivers meet in India and Bangladesh to form the world's largest delta. It is 300 miles (480 km) long and 100 miles (160 km) wide.

Delta

Waterfalls

Most **waterfalls** occur where hard bands of rock cross the bed of a river. The river wears aways the hard rock more slowly than softer rock downstream. Eventually this creates a steep drop.

● The world's highest waterfall is the Salto Angel Falls in Venezuela. It plunges down a cliff 3,212 ft. (979 m) high.

Strange but true

● A huge underground river runs underneath the Nile, with six times more water than the river above.

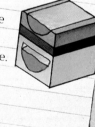

● Lake Bosumtwi in Ghana formed in a hollow made by a meteorite.

● Beaver Lake in Yellowstone Park was artificially created by beaver damming.

● The world's shortest river is the D River, Oregon. It is only 121 ft. (37 m.) long.

Oceans

There are four large oceans on the Earth. They join together to form one huge mass of water. They are called the **Pacific**, the **Atlantic**, the **Indian**, and the **Arctic**.

Parts of the oceans are divided into smaller areas called **seas**. These are mostly around coastlines and islands.

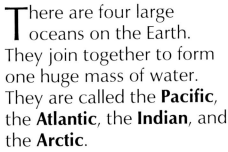

The **temperature** of seawater varies across the world. For instance, most of the water in the Arctic is permanently frozen, whereas in hot tropical areas the sea can reach the temperature of a warm bath.

Ocean floor profile

If you were able to look beneath the ocean surface you would see:

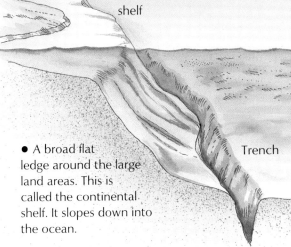

Continental shelf

Trench

- Deep valleys called submarine canyons, crossing the continental shelf.

- Very deep crevices called ocean trenches rimming the edges of some oceans. They mark places where one of the Earth's plates is moving beneath another (see p.8).

- A broad flat ledge around the large land areas. This is called the continental shelf. It slopes down into the ocean.

- A giant plain, called an abyssal plain, across the middle.

Tides

The **Moon's gravity** pulls on the Earth and draws the oceans into two bulges, one facing the Moon and one on the other side of the planet. The Moon drags these two bulges around with it as it circles the Earth causing daily **tides**.

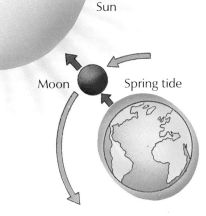

Sun

Moon

Spring tide

- Twice a month the Sun and Moon line up, and together their gravity pulls cause a very high "spring tide."

Coral reefs

Coral reefs are found in warm shallow seas. They are built by tiny animals called **polyps**. Each polyp builds a small stone cup to live in. When a polyp dies, it leaves its cup behind. New polyps build on top and gradually the reef grows.

Fringe reef

Barrier reef

- Fringe reefs grow around the shores of continents or islands.

- Barrier reefs grow several miles offshore. The Australian Great Barrier Reef is the biggest example.

- A coral atoll is a broken ring of coral islands with water in the middle.

Coral polyp

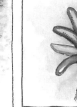
Coral atoll

Atlantic 31,660,000 sq. miles (82,000,000 sq. km)	**Indian** 28,350,000 sq. miles (73,426,000 sq. km)	**Arctic** 4,700,000 sq. miles (12,173,000 sq. km)

● A range of volcanic mountains called an oceanic ridge is found in some oceans. This is where the Earth's plates are pulling apart (see p.8).

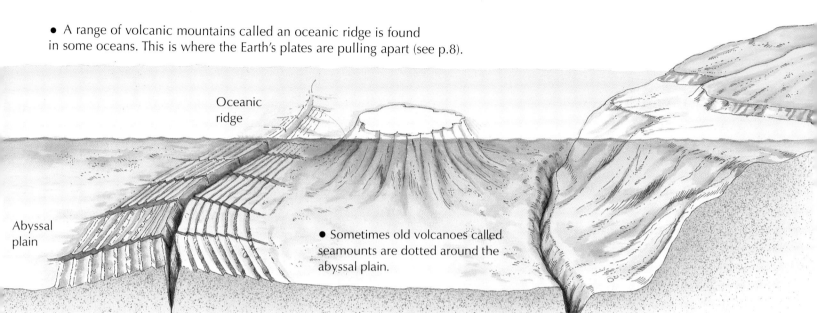

Oceanic ridge

Abyssal plain

● Sometimes old volcanoes called seamounts are dotted around the abyssal plain.

Sun

Neap tide

Moon

● When the Moon and Sun are at right angles the Sun opposes the Moon's gravity pull, causing a very low "neap tide."

Currents

Water near the ocean surface travels around the world in **currents**. These movements are caused by winds, differences in water temperature and saltiness, coastline shape and the Earth's rotation.

● The world's largest current is the West Wind Drift, which flows between America and Antarctica.

Strange but true

● Off the coast of Florida there is an underwater hotel. Guests have to dive to the entrance.

● There is one-seventh ounce (4 grams) of gold in every million tons of seawater.

● The biggest storm wave ever recorded was 111 ft. (34 m) high from crest to trough.

● Only about a ninth of an iceberg shows above the surface of the water.

Sea riches

● Oysters, seaweed, and fish can be farmed in the sea. Some scientists have managed to build artificial reef "farms" and colonize them with lobsters and shellfish.

● Underwater communities could be built for marine farm workers. Some experiments have already been carried out using prototype underwater houses.

● On the deep ocean floor there are millions of rock lumps called manganese nodules. Manganese is used for hardening steel.

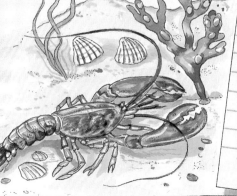

Rain Forests

Bananas

Rain forests are dense forests that grow in areas of **heavy rainfall** around the **equator**. They are found in West Africa, Southeast Asia, South America and the islands of the western Pacific.

Rain forests of the world

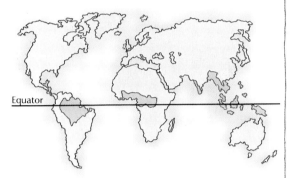

Equator

Rain forests provide a home for the widest variety of animals and plants to be found anywhere in the world. For instance, in just one small area of the **Amazon** rain forest in South America there are likely to be hundreds of different kinds of trees and animals.

Rain forest layers

Different types of **animals** and **plants** are found living at different heights in rain forest trees.

- Extra-tall trees called emergents grow above the rest of the jungle at heights between 145 and 200 ft. (45 and 60 m). Giant eagles nest in them.

- Lots of animals live in the canopy. This layer grows from about 100 to 150 ft. (30 to 45 m) high. It is rich in flowers and fruit.

- Ropelike plants called lianas grow up the tree trunks. Animals hang on to them to swing between branches.

200 ft.

130 ft.

65 ft.

15 ft.

- Small saplings and shrubs form the understory layer, rising to about 30 ft. (10 m) high.

- On the ground there is a thin layer of rotting leaves and vegetation called "leaf litter." It provides a home for many insects and fungi.

- The trees spread their roots out near the surface to gather all the food and moisture they can. Some of them grow big flat buttress roots to support their weight.

Rain forest plants

- Rain forest trees flower at different times. Many of them have bright petals and sweet nectar to attract birds and insects to pollinate them.

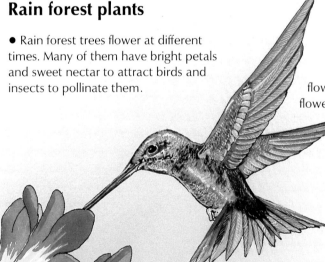

- In some rain forests hummingbirds feed on the nectar from flowers. They hover in front of a flower, beating their wings so fast that they make a humming noise. They dip their beaks into each bloom and suck out the nectar with their tongues.

- Many different plants festoon themselves around the forest trees, dangling their roots in the air to pick up moisture.

22

Rain forest animals

Mammals, **birds**, **fish**, **insects**, **amphibians**, and **reptiles** can all be found in the South American rain forests.

Jaguar

- Rain forest mammals include tree-living cats such as jaguars and margays.

- Jungle reptiles include lizards and snakes of all kinds and sizes.

Anaconda

- Jungle insects include ants, butterflies, termites, and beetles of all different kinds.

- Some jungle leaves collect pools of water that attract many kinds of tree frog. Most tree frogs have suckers on their hands and feet to anchor them securely to branches.

Tree frog

- Bright macaws, parrots, and toucans are just a few of the birds that nest in the jungle canopy.

Macaw

- Monkeys of all kinds swing from the jungle trees. Most South American monkeys have prehensile tails which they can use as an extra hand to grab onto things.

- Rain forests have rivers teeming with fish. The Amazon river is home to the ferocious piranha.

Piranha

Strange but true

- The goliath beetle is found in African jungles. It grows up to 6 inches (14 cm) long and when it flies it sounds like a small aircraft.

- Amazon army ants sometimes travel in groups up to 20 million strong. They destroy and eat everything in their path.

- Gibbon monkeys look acrobatic, but in fact many of them suffer from broken limbs through falling.

Rain forest people

The **people** who live in rain forests are usually grouped in small **tribes**.

- Some rain forest people survive by hunting for meat and gathering plants. They have a great knowledge of the rain forests and know exactly where to find food supplies.

- The traditional livelihoods of the rain forest Indians are increasingly threatened by forest clearing and mining projects. International efforts are being made to help them.

Deserts

Deserts are places where less than 10 inches (25 cm) of rain falls per year. Food and water are scarce in these inhospitable regions.

There are lots of different types of **desert landscape**, ranging from sand dunes to rocky plains and mountains. Desert edges have more rain and are sometimes called semi-desert.

Deserts occur for several reasons. Some deserts are so far from the sea that by the time wind reaches them, all the moisture in the air has gone.

Some deserts are dry because they are near mountains. All the moisture in the air falls as rain and snow on the mountain tops before it reaches the desert on the other side.

Deserts of the world

The world's main **desert areas** are shown below:

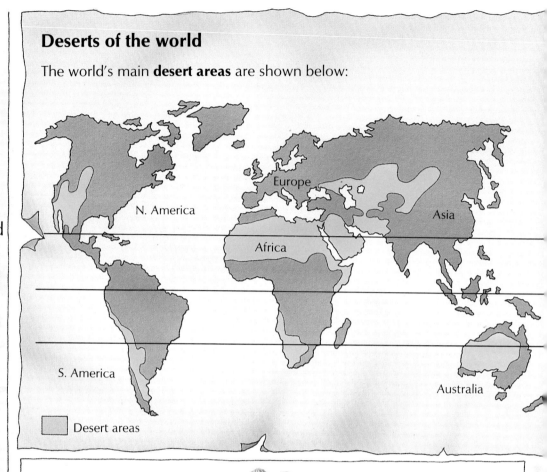

N. America

Europe

Asia

Africa

S. America

Australia

☐ Desert areas

Desert plants

Desert plants are adapted to drought:

● They gather water through their roots, which either spread out near the surface to soak up dew or grow deep down to moist soil layers.

● Some cacti have pleated skins that stretch so they can store water.

● The biggest cactus is the saguaro, found in the Sonoran Desert in southwest U.S.A. It can grow to 50 ft. (15 m) high.

● Many desert plants only flower and seed themselves when rains come. The plant seeds then lie in the ground for years until the next rain shower comes along.

Desert flower

Saguaro cactus

● Desert plants often have bright beautiful flowers that only appear for a short time after rain has fallen. They don't live long, so they must attract pollinating insects quickly. That is why their petals are so colorful.

24

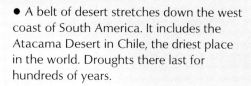

Seif   Star-shaped   Transverse

Parallel

• North American deserts have rocky plains, deep ravines, salt lakes, and canyons. The hottest place is Death Valley, California, where temperatures can reach over 130°F (56°C).

• The North African Sahara is the world's biggest desert, covering an area almost the size of the U.S. Most of it is rocky. Only about a tenth of it is covered in sand dunes.

• A belt of desert stretches down the west coast of South America. It includes the Atacama Desert in Chile, the driest place in the world. Droughts there last for hundreds of years.

• Much of central Australia is a semi-desert called the Outback. It is dotted with rocky outcrops such as the famous Ayers Rock.

Ayers Rock

• The Arabian Desert is partly a sea of sand with dunes up to 800 ft. (240 m) high. Bedouin tribes travel the desert, camping in tents wherever they stop.

• The Gobi Desert in central Asia has hot summers and severe winters. The people who live there are nomads. They spend their lives traveling the barren, rocky land in search of grazing for their yak herds.

Yak and tribesman

• The Kalahari Desert in southern Africa is on a huge plateau. In the middle there is a sea of red sand dunes. The Kalahari bushmen hunt and gather food from this wilderness.

Kalahari bushman

Desert animals

Desert animals usually shelter during the heat of the day and come out when the temperature drops in the evening. They get the moisture they need from eating plants or other creatures.

• Most desert spiders do not build webs. Instead they hunt for food. The camel spider is one of the largest desert specimens. It spans up to 6 inches (15 cm).

• Camels can survive for many days without water. Their nostrils can close up to keep out the dust.

• Desert reptiles include all kinds of snakes and lizards. They stay in the shade when they can.

Strange but true

• Prehistoric paintings show the Sahara as fertile land.

• Early European explorers of the Australian Outback took a boat with them. They were looking for a fabled lake.

• In Saudi Arabia there are solar-powered pay phones in the desert.

• Ostriches sometimes eat sand, probably to help their digestion.

25

Polar Regions

The **Arctic** and the **Antarctic** are the coldest regions in the world.

The Arctic is the area inside the **Arctic Circle**, which is a line of latitude below the North Pole. The **Arctic Ocean** is in the middle, and is frozen in winter. The land around the edge is **tundra**.

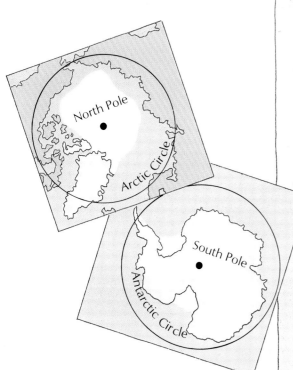

The **Antarctic** is a continent surrounding the South Pole. It covers over 9 percent of the Earth's surface.

Most of the Antarctic land is covered by a thick sheet of ice. Wildlife is found only around the coasts and on outlying islands, where the temperature is warmer than it is inland.

The Arctic

For most of the year, the Arctic **tundra** is covered in snow. In the brief summer months the snow melts, but cannot drain away because under the land surface there is a permanently frozen layer of the earth called **permafrost**. Instead, the water gathers in lakes, pools, and bogs.

- Sometimes the wind whips up the Arctic snow and causes "white outs" which are rather like sandstorms in the desert. White outs can start suddenly and last for days.

- Most Arctic animals are to be found on the tundra. They arrive in summer and migrate south or hibernate underground in winter.

- Tundra plants are small. They grow near the ground to avoid the biting winds and cold temperatures. Some of them have hairy stems that help to keep them warm.

The Antarctic

The Antarctic is the **coldest** and **windiest** place on Earth. Its ice sheets hold a large amount of the Earth's permanent ice. In the Antarctic:

- The tops of high mountains only just peek above the ice, which is up to $2\frac{1}{2}$ miles (4 km) thick in parts.

- The world's biggest icebergs, up to 60 miles (100 km) wide, break off from the coastal ice shelf and drift far out to sea. This process of breaking off is called "calving."

- Some areas of coastal land are exposed in summer. Algae and lichen grow here, but there are hardly any other plants.

Killer whale

Minke whale

Humpback whale

- Many Arctic animals have white fur, which camouflages them against snow. For instance, the Arctic hare is very hard to spot against a wintery background.

Arctic hare

- The coat of the Arctic caribou is ideal for keeping warm. Each hair is hollow so that it can trap warm air inside.

Caribou

- Some Arctic animals are plant eaters and some are hunters. The polar bear is the fiercest of them all. Its main prey is the ringed seal.

Polar bear

- The Arctic is already being used for natural resources such as oil. Its development must be planned very carefully, so as not to damage the lives of its unique animals.

Strange but true

- The biggest animal found on inland Antarctica is the housefly.

- The Antarctic notothenia fish has a protein in its blood that acts like antifreeze and stops the fish freezing in icy sea.

- Penguins are so well insulated by fat that they often overheat when they are active. They have to stand with their beaks open to cool down.

- The Adelie penguin can leap four times its own height to get from sea to land.

Life in the Antarctic

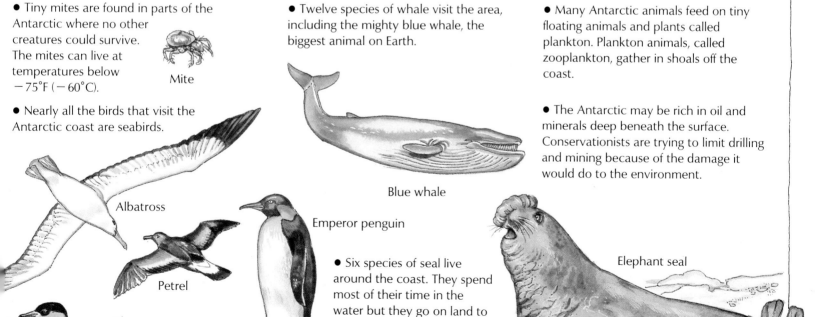

- Tiny mites are found in parts of the Antarctic where no other creatures could survive. The mites can live at temperatures below $-75°F$ ($-60°C$).

Mite

- Nearly all the birds that visit the Antarctic coast are seabirds.

Albatross

Petrel

Skua

Emperor penguin

- Twelve species of whale visit the area, including the mighty blue whale, the biggest animal on Earth.

Blue whale

- Six species of seal live around the coast. They spend most of their time in the water but they go on land to breed.

- Many Antarctic animals feed on tiny floating animals and plants called plankton. Plankton animals, called zooplankton, gather in shoals off the coast.

- The Antarctic may be rich in oil and minerals deep beneath the surface. Conservationists are trying to limit drilling and mining because of the damage it would do to the environment.

Elephant seal

The Universe

The universe goes on for ever. Most of it is **empty space**, with huge swarms of stars called **galaxies** shining out into the blackness. Our Sun belongs to a galaxy called the **Milky Way** containing about 100 billion stars. There are billions of galaxies in the universe.

Our Sun is a star. Other stars may also have planets, comets, and other space bodies circling around them. There are probably other planets like the Earth in the universe.

The Solar System

The **Solar System** is the name given to our Sun and all the space bodies that revolve around it, including the Earth.

● There are nine planets and over 60 moons, or satellites, all spinning as they orbit or travel around the Sun.

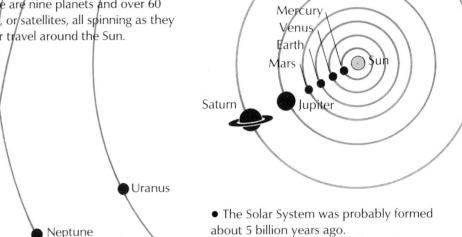

Mercury
Venus
Earth
Mars
Sun
Saturn
Jupiter
Uranus
Neptune
Pluto

● The Solar System was probably formed about 5 billion years ago.

The Big Bang theory

Most scientists believe the universe began about 14 billion years ago with a gigantic explosion they call the **Big Bang**.

● The bang blasted hot material out in all directions. It was far hotter than a nuclear explosion, or even the center of the Sun.

● As this material cooled, it turned into hydrogen and helium. These are the two most common "elements," or substances, found in the universe.

● Galaxies and stars began to form out of hydrogen and helium about a billion years after the Big Bang.

Clues to the Big Bang

There are some **clues** to show that the Big Bang happened. Two of the most important clues are:

● The galaxies are flying farther apart, as if from the force of an explosion.

● Space is still slightly "warm" from the last traces of the explosion.

Theories about the future

There are **two main theories** about what will happen to the universe in the future. They are:

- The Open Theory, which says that the universe started with the Big Bang and the galaxies will carry on expanding for ever.

- The Closed Theory, which says that the universe will stop expanding. The pulling force of gravity will slowly drag the galaxies back toward each other again until there is a Big Crunch!

- The latest observations made by astronomers show that the Open Theory is more likely to be the correct one.

Earth

Gravity

Moon

Gravity

Gravity is the **pulling force** that exists between things. It is the force that keeps the Moon revolving around the Earth.

- The Sun's gravity keeps the planets in orbit, and stops them from flying off into space as they spin around.

- The Sun has a much greater pull of gravity than the Earth, because it has 333,000 times as much mass (amount of material) as Earth.

- Your weight is the force of the Earth's gravity pulling you down onto its surface.

Strange but true

- The temperature when the Big Bang happened was about 1 billion billion billion °C.

- A hundredth of a second later (the time needed to take a snapshot), it had cooled to 1 billion °C.

- Most of the material in the universe is invisible. Some of it may exist as dark particles between galaxies.

Measuring Space

Distances in space are too vast to be measured in miles, so scientists measure in **light-years**. A light-year is 5.88 trillion miles (9.46 trillion km) — the distance traveled by light in one year.

- The nearest star to the Sun is called Proxima Centauri. It is 4.3 light-years away, which means it takes 4.3 years for its light to reach Earth.

Hubble space telescope

Radio telescope

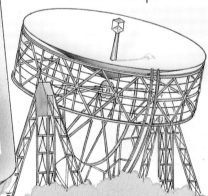

How far can we see?

- Radio telescopes on Earth have helped astronomers to detect very distant objects. The most distant galaxy so far observed by astronomers is at least 6 billion light-years away.

- Some telescopes have been put into Space. They can "see" more clearly than telescopes on Earth and can detect invisible energy waves (see p.31). One day they may discover new stars and planets.

The Stars

The stars in the sky look small because they are so far away. In fact they are huge. Each star is a glowing **ball of gases** held together by gravity. Most of this gas is **hydrogen**. In the hot fury of a star's "core" or center, hydrogen reaches a temperature of at least 18 million°F (10 million°C).

Every element consists of tiny atoms. The heat inside a star changes hydrogen atoms into the atoms of another gas called **helium**.

When this happens there is an **"atomic reaction"** and a flash of energy is given out. Billions of these flashes of energy keep the star hot and make it shine.

The **Sun** is the nearest star to Earth. It is only a middle-sized star but it looks big to us because it is so close — only 93 million miles (150 million km) away!

The birth and death of a star

Stars are born in clusters. A **cloud of gas and dust** called a **nebula** breaks up over millions of years into smaller clouds which are then pulled tighter and smaller by their own gravity. Eventually they heat up and start to shine.

A star being formed from gas and dust.

Gravity

Core

Gravity

● After billions of years, stars finally run out of energy and die.

Supernova

Red giant

● The remains of a very large star may collapse to form a black hole.

● Larger stars do not last as long as smaller ones. They die dramatically in an explosion. The exploding star is called a supernova.

● As a star grows old, its core becomes hotter and swells up. This swollen star is called a red giant.

Black hole

Pulsar

White dwarf

● A very small, extremely dense body is left, called a neutron star.

● A black hole is invisible because light cannot escape from it.

● Some neutron stars, called pulsars, give off pulses of light and radio waves as they spin.

● Eventually the star collapses and becomes a white dwarf — a small but very hot star. It cools and finally fades away.

The electromagnetic spectrum

Stars give off different kinds of **energy waves**, or **radiation**. Each kind has a different wavelength. Together they are called the **electromagnetic spectrum**.

● We can see one kind of energy wave — visible light. The others are invisible.

● Special instruments are used to detect radiation. Dangerous X rays and gamma rays are blocked by the Earth's atmosphere and have to be studied from space.

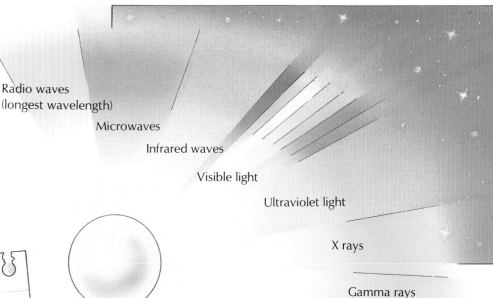

Radio waves (longest wavelength)

Microwaves

Infrared waves

Visible light

Ultraviolet light

X rays

Gamma rays (shortest wavelength)

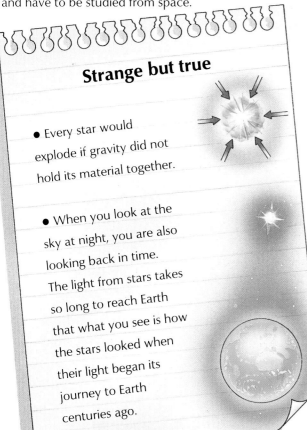

Strange but true

● Every star would explode if gravity did not hold its material together.

● When you look at the sky at night, you are also looking back in time. The light from stars takes so long to reach Earth that what you see is how the stars looked when their light began its journey to Earth centuries ago.

Different kinds of stars

Some stars, like the Sun, shine with a **steady light**. Other kinds of stars don't shine steadily. They are called **variable stars**.

● Some stars have a regular cycle of fading and getting brighter. For example, the star called Delta Cephei reaches full brightness every 5 days 9 hours.

● Some variable stars are really binary systems — two steadily shining stars orbiting each other. They seem to fade when one blocks light from the other and brighten when they are both visible at the same time.

● Sometimes a binary system star blazes very brightly for just a few nights. This is called a nova. It probably happens when a cloud of gas from one star explodes as it reaches the other star.

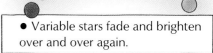

● Variable stars fade and brighten over and over again.

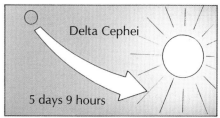

Delta Cephei

5 days 9 hours

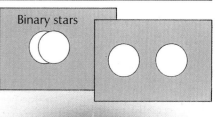

Binary stars

Nova

The Sun as a star

Sun

The Sun was formed from a **nebula** about 5 billion years ago, and will burn for about another 5 billion years.

● The Sun is the source of life on Earth. Without its light and heat, Earth would be dead and icy. (You can find out more about the Sun on pages 32–33).

The Sun

The Sun, like all stars, is a ball of fiercely **hot gas**. Hydrogen gas deep inside it is constantly being turned into helium (see p.30). This releases energy in the form of **light** and **heat**.

The Sun is the nearest star to Earth. In space terms it is relatively close—only about 93 million miles (150 million km) away!

The Sun has shone steadily for thousands of millions of years. If it went dim for only a few days, most life-forms on Earth would perish.

Features of the Sun

These are some of the Sun's more **spectacular features**:

● Enormous eruptions of gas, called prominences, rise continually from the surface of the Sun. Some reach out into Space as far as 1.2 million miles (2 million km).

Arched prominences

Sunspots

● Sunspots are darker, cooler areas that appear on the Sun's surface from time to time. Some are much larger than the Earth and can last for months. Smaller ones last for only a few days or weeks.

● Every 11 years or so, sunspots become more common and then fade away. This is called the sunspot cycle.

Solar flares

● Solar flares are violent explosions of energy from the Sun's surface. They shoot particles at high speed out into space. On Earth they can produce strange effects, such as the glowing lights, called aurorae, that sometimes appear in the night sky.

Sun facts

● The diameter of the Sun is 865,000 miles (1,392,000 km).

● The temperature at the core is believed to be about 25 million °F (14 million °C). At the surface it is 11,000°F (6,000°C).

● A million bodies the size of the Earth could be squashed inside the Sun.

● The Sun is 92 percent hydrogen. At the center is a core of helium. Around this core 4 million tons of the Sun's material is turned into energy every second.

Different parts of the Sun rotate at different speeds.

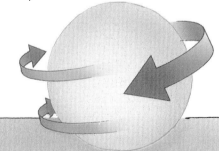

Different speeds

● Because the Sun is made of gases, different parts of it can rotate at different speeds. The center part, or equator area, rotates faster than the poles.

● Energy from the core takes a million years to reach the Sun's surface, but only $8\frac{1}{2}$ minutes to travel from the Sun's surface to the Earth.

Chromosphere — a layer a few thousand miles deep that shines pink during an eclipse

Corona — the outer atmosphere that stretches millions of miles into space

WARNING Never look directly at the Sun. It can damage your eyes and blind you.

Solar eclipses

Occasionally the **Moon** passes in front of the Sun so that it **blocks out sunlight** from part of the Earth. This is called a **total solar eclipse**.

● If the eclipse is total, the Sun's faint atmosphere or corona shines out in the darkened sky. This is the only time it can be seen from Earth.

● During a total eclipse, prominences can sometimes be seen flaring out around the darkened outline of the Sun. Eclipses provide scientists with good opportunities for studying such things as prominences and the corona.

● When the Moon blocks out only part of the Sun's light, this is called a partial eclipse.

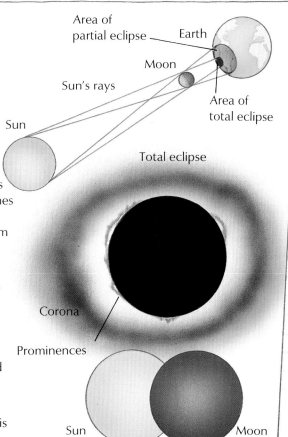

Area of partial eclipse

Earth

Moon

Sun's rays

Area of total eclipse

Sun

Total eclipse

Corona

Prominences

Sun

Moon

Partial eclipse

Strange but true

● The Sun is described by scientists as a yellow dwarf star.

● There may be a connection between the appearance of sunspots and changes in the weather on Earth.

● Sound waves produced inside the Sun make it swell and shrink by a mile or so every few minutes.

What will happen to the Sun?

Like all stars, the Sun is **changing**. This is what scientists believe will happen to it:

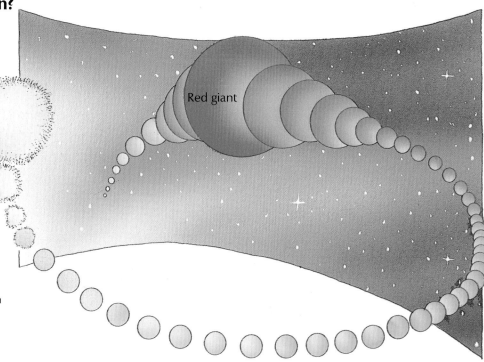

Red giant

1. Several billion years from now, the Sun will have a crisis. The hydrogen supply around its core will start to run out, and our star will begin to collapse.

2. This collapse will put new energy into the core so the Sun will blaze hotter than ever.

3. The blast of energy will force the higher gas layers outward. The Sun will become a red giant, 100 times its present diameter and 500 times brighter.

4. The red giant will fill Earth's sky. The great heat will melt the surface of the Earth into seas of lava.

5. Eventually, the Sun will cool and shrink, becoming a white dwarf star (see p.30) about the size of the Earth.

The Moon

 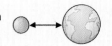
The Moon is an airless ball of **rock** about a quarter the diameter of the Earth. It circles around the Earth once every 27.3 days. It has no **light** of its own, but reflects light from the Sun.

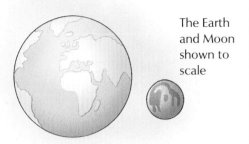

The Earth and Moon shown to scale

The Moon has probably always been lifeless, but it has had a violent, turbulent history. Most of the **craters** on its surface were caused by solid space bodies called meteoroids crashing into it between 3 and 4 billion years ago. The darker areas are called **maria** (seas). They are made of lava that flowed out from inside the Moon about 3 billion years ago.

Gravity

The Moon is much smaller than Earth and so has much weaker **gravity**. Astronauts had to be weighted down to help them walk properly on the Moon's surface.

Astronauts on the Moon

- It is gravity that causes ocean tides on Earth to rise and fall. The gravity of the Sun and Moon pulls the Earth's oceans into bulges. The Earth rotates beneath these bulges, producing two high tides a day.

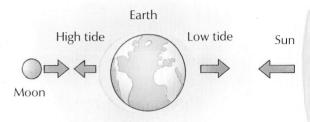

Phases of the Moon

The Moon keeps the same **side** facing Earth all the time, so we only see this one side of it. As the Moon travels around the Earth, we see a varying amount of this side each day, depending on how much of it is sunlit. These different amounts, or stages, are called the **phases of the Moon**.

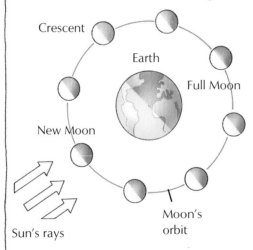

- When the Moon is seen as a crescent, only a sliver of the side facing Earth is sunlit.

- As the Moon moves around the Earth, it appears half-lit and then finally fully lit (the Full Moon). At this stage the whole of the side facing Earth is sunlit.

- After Full Moon, the shape changes back to half and finally to a thin crescent. It then disappears for a few nights (New Moon) and the process begins again.

- It takes 29.5 days for the Moon to move through all its phases from New, through Full, and back to New again.

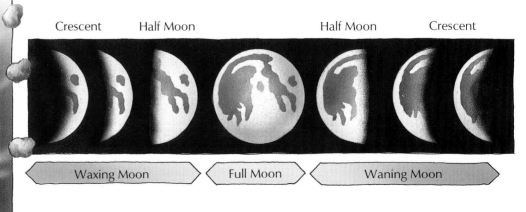

- As the Moon grows from crescent to Full, it is called the waxing moon.

- As it shrinks back to a crescent, it is called the waning moon.

The Moon's surface

The Moon's **surface** is covered with craters, ridges, mountains, and valleys. The dark maria are the smoothest parts because the lava that created them flowed over and covered old craters. These are some facts about the Moon's surface:

● The biggest Moon crater that can be seen from Earth is called Bailly. It is about 180 miles (290 km) across.

● The largest Moon crater is on the far side of the Moon and so cannot be seen from Earth.

● Because the Moon has no air or water to wear rocks away, the Moon's surface has remained unchanged for thousands of millions of years.

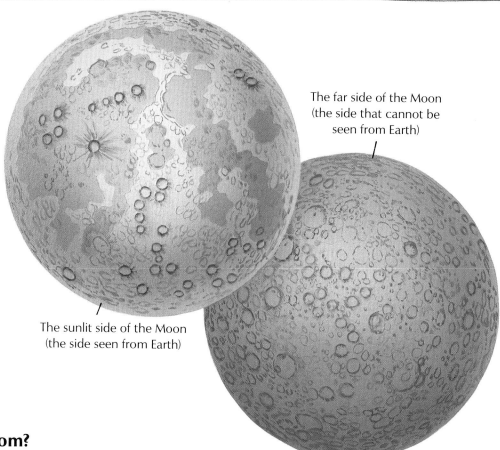

The far side of the Moon (the side that cannot be seen from Earth)

The sunlit side of the Moon (the side seen from Earth)

Where did the Moon come from?

The Moon and Earth are roughly the same age. Scientists are unsure where the Moon came from. Here are four theories:

1. The Moon and Earth formed together from the same dust and gas cloud.

2. The Moon was a wandering space body that came close to Earth and became trapped in Earth's orbit.

3. When the Earth was young and molten, it grew a bulge that spun off and became the Moon.

4. A small planet hit the young molten Earth and threw material into orbit, which got drawn together to form the Moon.

Strange but true

● The Moon is moving slowly away from Earth at the rate of an inch per year.

● The far side of the Moon was not seen until 1959 when the Soviet spacecraft Luna 3 flew by and took pictures of it.

● Earth's gravity has pulled on the side of the Moon that faces Earth, causing a bulge several miles high.

● It would take 81 Moons to weigh the same as Earth.

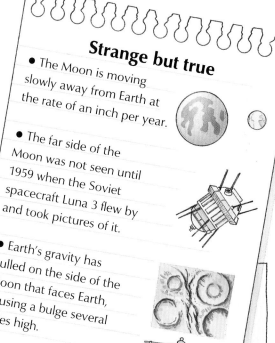

Lunar eclipses

The Earth casts a long **shadow** in space on the side away from the Sun. A **lunar eclipse** happens when the Moon passes into the darkest part of this shadow. During a total lunar eclipse, the Moon looks a dark red-brown color.

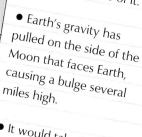

Sun

Earth

Moon

Earth's shadow

Earth and the Solar System

Earth is a smallish, rocky planet. It is in just the right place in the Solar System to allow **life** to be supported. If Earth were nearer to the Sun, it would be too hot for life as we know it to survive. If it were farther away, it would be too cold.

Seen from space, Earth is a beautiful **bluish disk** with swirling white clouds. It looks blue because so much of its surface is ocean.

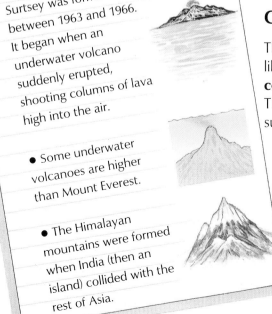

Earth seen from space

Earth's position in the Solar System

Earth is the third planet from the Sun. Its closest neighbors are Venus and Mars.

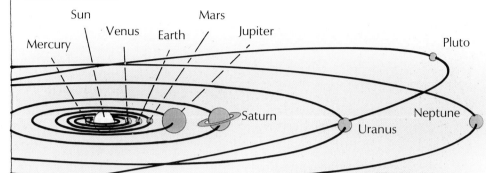

How the Earth began

Earth was formed about 4.6 billion years ago, from **small rocky bodies** that collided with each other as they whirled around the Sun.

● These collisions gave out so much energy that the Earth glowed red-hot as farther rocky bodies crashed into it.

● After several hundred million years, Earth reached its present size. The collisions died down and the Earth started to cool.

● The metal in the Earth sank to the center, forming the core, with the lighter rocks forming the mantle and crust.

Crust, mantle, and core

This is what the Earth might look like inside. At the center is the **core**, surrounded by the **mantle**. The **crust** is a thin layer on the surface.

● The Earth's core is about 4,500 miles (7,000 km) across and is probably made of iron and nickel. The outer part is liquid and the inner part solid.

● The mantle is made of rock. It contains most of the Earth's material.

● The crust is made of lighter rocks that floated to the top when Earth was molten. It varies from 4 to 25 miles (6 to 40 km) thick.

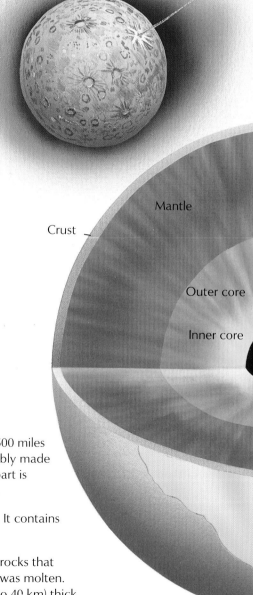

Mantle

Crust

Outer core

Inner core

Strange but true

● The Icelandic island of Surtsey was formed between 1963 and 1966. It began when an underwater volcano suddenly erupted, shooting columns of lava high into the air.

● Some underwater volcanoes are higher than Mount Everest.

● The Himalayan mountains were formed when India (then an island) collided with the rest of Asia.

Earth's atmosphere

Earth is surrounded by an **atmosphere**, which enables life to survive on the planet. This is what the atmosphere does:

● Provides the air we breathe.

● Protects Earth from harmful rays from Space (see p.31).

● Protects Earth from space debris, such as meteors.

● Stops Earth getting too cold at night or too hot in the day.

Layers of the atmosphere

The atmosphere can be divided into these **different layers**:

● Exosphere (300–5,000 miles (500–8,000 km) above the Earth) Weather satellites orbit in this layer.

● Ionosphere (50–300 miles (80–500 km) above the Earth) This layer protects the Earth from harmful rays.

● Mesosphere (30–50 miles (48–80 km) above the Earth) Unmanned balloons have measured the temperature of this layer.

● Stratosphere (6–30 miles (10–48 km) above the Earth) Jet aircraft fly in this layer.

● The ozone layer is part of the stratosphere, at about 25 miles (40 km) high.

● Troposphere (From the ground to 6 miles (10 km) high) We live in this layer and all Earth's weather happens in it.

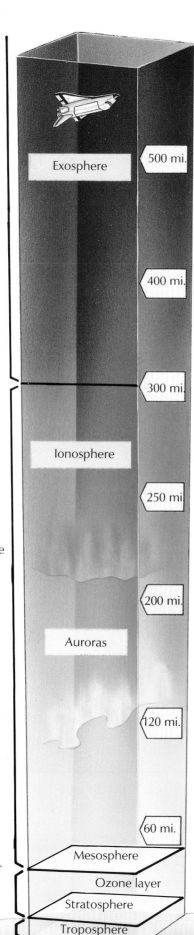

Exosphere — 500 mi.
— 400 mi.
— 300 mi.
Ionosphere — 250 mi.
— 200 mi.
Auroras — 120 mi.
— 60 mi.
Mesosphere
Ozone layer
Stratosphere
Troposphere

Volcanoes

Volcanoes are openings in the Earth's crust where melted rock from inside bursts through to the surface. Some melted rock (called **lava**) spills out. It can build up around the opening to form a **mountain**.

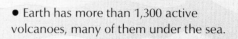

Lava

Molten rock

● Earth has more than 1,300 active volcanoes, many of them under the sea.

● The islands of Hawaii and Iceland are made of rock that erupted out of the sea from underwater volcanoes.

● Most volcanoes are found near where the plates of the Earth's crust (see below) collide with each other.

Plates

The Earth's **crust** in not an unbroken shell. It is a jigsaw of about 15 huge **rocky pieces** called **plates** that continually push and slide against each other.

● When two plates collide, the rocks they are made of can get squashed and pushed up into the air. Some mountains were formed that way.

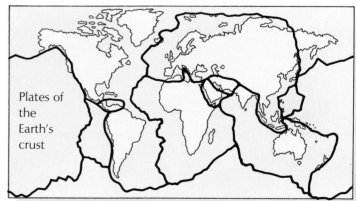

Plates of the Earth's crust

● Earthquakes are caused by the plates of the Earth's crust sliding against each other.

● The surface of the Earth is changing all the time as rocks wear down and plates move.

The Nearest Planets

The nearest planets to Earth are **Mercury**, **Venus**, and **Mars**. They all have a solid, **rocky surface**, like Earth's.

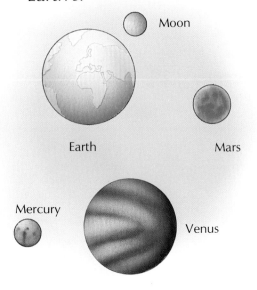

Moon

Earth

Mars

Mercury

Venus

Space probes have taken photographs of Venus, Mars, and Mercury and studied their surfaces. Some people thought there was a slight chance of finding **life** on Mars, but no sign of life was found on any of these planets.

Mercury facts

Mercury is the **closest planet** to the Sun. It has:

● Extremely hot days, with temperatures of 650°F (350°C), because it is so close to the Sun.

● Very cold nights, because there is no atmosphere to trap the daytime heat.

● An iron core, like the Earth's.

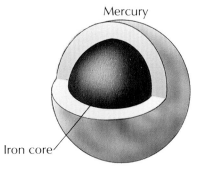

Mercury

Iron core

● Earth is $2\frac{1}{2}$ times bigger than Mercury.

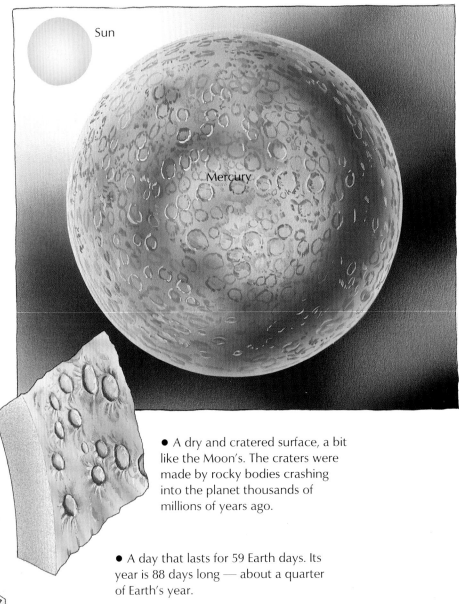

Sun

Mercury

● A dry and cratered surface, a bit like the Moon's. The craters were made by rocky bodies crashing into the planet thousands of millions of years ago.

● A day that lasts for 59 Earth days. Its year is 88 days long — about a quarter of Earth's year.

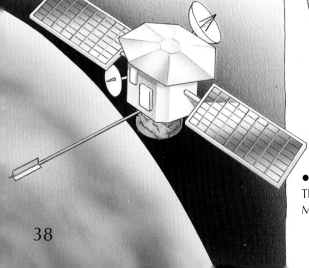

● Mercury spins around the Sun faster than any other planet. This is how it came by its name. In Ancient Greek mythology, Mercury was the swift messenger of the gods.

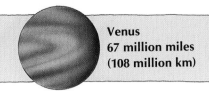

Venus
67 million miles
(108 million km)

Earth
93 million miles
(150 million km)

Mars
142 million miles
(228 million km)

Venus facts

Venus (named after the goddess of love) is the closest planet to Earth and shines more brightly than any other planet. It has:

● Heavy, swirling clouds that hide the mountains and craters on its surface. The clouds trap the Sun's heat, raising the temperature to around 900°F (480°C).

● Three large highland areas surrounded by deserts. These have been seen only by radar, as clouds cover them from view.

● An atmosphere of mainly unbreatheable carbon dioxide. There are constant thunderstorms, with drops of sulfuric acid in the clouds.

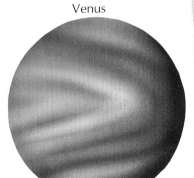

Venus

● Venus is similar in size to the Earth.

● Ishtar Terra, a highland area of Venus, is larger than the U.S.A.

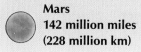

Strange but true

● Venus's day is very long. It takes 243 days to spin once, and only 224 days to go around the Sun.

● Clouds on Venus spin around the planet in only four days.

● Mars has a volcano, called Olympus Mons, that stretches 15 miles (25 km) above the planet's surface. It is the largest volcano in the Solar System.

Mars facts

Mars is the farthest inner planet from the Sun. It looks red from Earth, which is why it was named after Mars, the god of war. Mars has:

● A barren, dusty surface with reddish soil and rocks. There are deep canyons and high volcanoes.

● A day that lasts for 24 hours, 37 minutes — almost the same as Earth's. Its year, however, is nearly twice as long as Earth's — 687 days.

● A thin atmosphere of carbon dioxide that does not block the Sun's harmful radiation. It is cold, with temperatures averaging −9°C (−23°C).

● Occasional large dust storms that are visible through a telescope from Earth.

● Spectacular white icy caps at its north and south poles. These grow and shrink depending on the Martian seasons.

● A long time ago, some astronomers thought there might be intelligent life on Mars because regular lines on the planet's surface looked as if they had been made by intelligent beings.

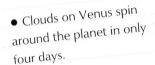

Mars's surface

● Mars has two very small natural satellites, or moons, called Phobos and Deimos. Phobos is 14 miles (22 km) across. Deimos is 9 miles (14 km) across.

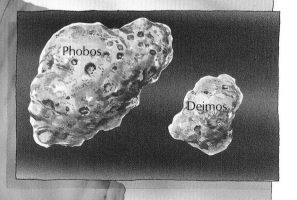

Phobos

Deimos

The Giant Planets

The giant planets, **Jupiter** and **Saturn**, are the largest planets in the Solar System. Their surfaces are not solid and rocky but are made up of a mixture of turbulent, swirling **gas** and **ice**.

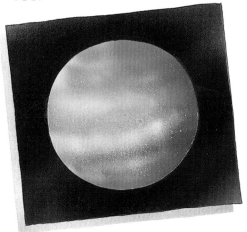

Jupiter

Jupiter, the biggest planet, is so huge that all the other planets in the Solar System could fit inside it.

Saturn

Saturn is smaller than Jupiter, but is very large. It is surrounded by brightly shining rings.

Jupiter facts

● Its day is only 9 hours 50 minutes long (the time it takes to spin around once).

● Its year is 11.9 Earth years long (the time it takes to circle around the Sun).

● Its diameter (through the Equator) is about 88,700 miles (142,800 km).

● There is a very faint ring around it, made of rocky particles. The ring is too faint to be seen from Earth.

● Its atmosphere is made of hydrogen and helium.

Inside Jupiter

Jupiter is made mainly of **hydrogen**. Its four major layers are:

● A very small rocky core

● An inner layer of hydrogen

● A shell of liquid hydrogen and helium

● A swirling surface of icy clouds

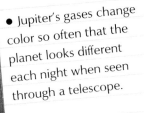

Strange but true

● Jupiter's gases change color so often that the planet looks different each night when seen through a telescope.

● Until the Voyager 1 space probe passed it in 1979, astronomers did not know Jupiter had a ring around it.

● Winds on Saturn blow at about 900 mph (1,400 km/h). Tornadoes on Earth blow at only 180–400 mph (300–600 km/h).

The Great Red Spot

Jupiter's **Great Red Spot** is a swirling **tornado** that has been raging for at least 100 years. It is about 25,000 miles (40,000 km) long and 7,000 miles (11,000 km) wide. That is more than three times the diameter of Earth!

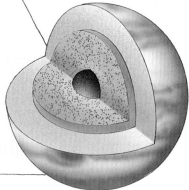

Saturn's rings

Saturn's **rings** are **bands of ice** and **rock** whirling around the planet. The largest rocks are several yards across.

● There are three main rings containing thousands of separate ringlets.

● Saturn's rings are huge but very thin. A sheet of paper 12 feet across would give you a scale model of their depth (the thickness of the paper) compared to their width (the width of the paper).

Voyager space probe

● Voyager probes photographed Saturn's rings and found new satellites

Saturn facts

● Its day (the time it takes to spin around once) is only 10 hours 14 minutes long.

● Its year (the time it takes to circle around the Sun) is 29.5 Earth years.

● Its diameter (across the Equator) is about 75,000 miles (120,000 km).

● Its diameter measured from one side of the ring system to the other is 169,000 miles (272,000 km).

● Its atmosphere is made of hydrogen and helium.

● A bright white area appeared on the surface in September 1990. It is as large as Jupiter's Great Red Spot.

The satellites

Jupiter and Saturn have natural **satellites**, or **moons**, orbiting them. Jupiter has at least 16 moons and Saturn at least 18.

Jupiter's main satellites

● Callisto, the outermost, is an icy and cratered satellite much bigger than Earth's Moon.

● Ganymede is larger than the planet Mercury. Its surface is icy, with grooves and streaks.

● Europa is smaller than Earth's Moon. It is smooth and icy with very few craters.

● Io, the innermost, is slightly larger than the Moon. It has a red, volcanic surface.

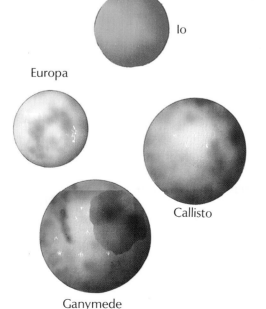

Io

Europa

Callisto

Ganymede

Some of Saturn's satellites

● Mimas (pictured below) is one of the innermost satellites. It has a crater on its surface over 60 miles (100 km) wide. That is nearly two-thirds of its diameter!

● Titan, the largest satellite, is bigger than Mercury. It has a cloudy atmosphere of nitrogen gas, and may have oceans made of liquid methane.

Uranus, Neptune, and Pluto

Uranus, Neptune, and Pluto are the **farthest planets** from the Sun. They are all icy cold. Uranus and Neptune are quite similar to each other and look greenish in color from Earth. Pluto, the tiniest of all the planets, is a dim speck.

In 1985 and 1989, the space probe **Voyager 2** flew past Uranus and Neptune. It took spectacular pictures of the planets, showing details never seen before. It also showed the **rings** around both planets, and discovered an amazing number of new **satellites** — ten for Uranus and six for Neptune.

Uranus

Uranus was discovered in 1781 by **William Herschel**, an amateur astronomer, using a homemade telescope. At first he thought he had found a comet.

Uranus

● Uranus is made up mostly of hydrogen and helium. The gas methane is also present in its atmosphere, which makes Uranus look green from Earth.

Uranus's satellites

Uranus has 15 satellites altogether. The five main ones are Miranda, Ariel, Umbriel, Titania, and Oberon. The largest, Oberon and Titania, are about 900 miles (1,500 km) across.

Umbriel   Oberon
Ariel
Miranda   Titania

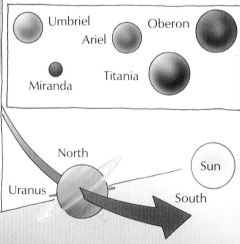

North
Uranus   Sun
South

● Uranus spins on its side instead of almost upright, like the other planets. Because of this, the poles of the planet can sometimes face the Sun. When this happens, they are warmer than the Earth's equator!

● The diameter of Uranus is 32,300 miles (52,000 km). Its day is about 17 hours long, and it takes 84 years to travel around the Sun.

Herschel's telescope

● Until 1986, only nine rings had been counted around Uranus. On its fly-past, however, Voyager 2 found four more rings, making 13 in all.

Strange but true

● Uranus's small satellite, Miranda, may have been shattered in a collision with another body. It seems to have broken up into large pieces which collected together again.

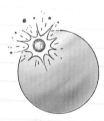

● The cycle of seasons on Triton, Neptune's largest satellite, takes 680 years.

● During the 1990s, Pluto is the nearest it can get to Earth, so it is a very good time to study it. This will not happen again until the 23rd century!

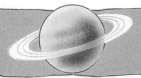

Neptune

Neptune was discovered in 1846. It cannot be seen with the naked eye. Through a telescope it looks like a faint blue-green star. Like Uranus, it is surrounded by **rings**.

- Neptune is colder than Uranus. It is about − 360°F (− 220°C).

- Neptune is slightly smaller than Uranus, measuring 30,000 miles (48,400 km) across.

Triton

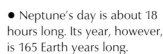

Neptune

- Neptune's day is about 18 hours long. Its year, however, is 165 Earth years long.

Neptune's satellites

Neptune has **eight satellites**. The two main ones are called Triton and Nereid. Triton, the larger, is smaller than Earth's Moon. Very unusually it orbits Neptune in the opposite direction from the planet's own spin.

Nereid

Pluto

Pluto is the **smallest planet**. Because of its orbit (see below) it is usually the farthest away from the Sun. It was not discovered until 1930 and is very difficult to see, even with a telescope.

Pluto

- Pluto's diameter is 1,800 miles (3,000 km) which means it is smaller than the Moon.

- Pluto's day lasts for just over six Earth days, and its year lasts 248 Earth years.

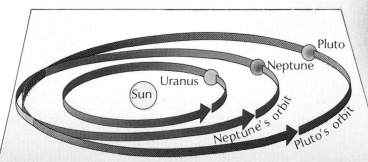

- Pluto is usually the farthest planet from the Sun. However, its orbit sometimes takes it inside Neptune's orbit. This is happening now, so from 1979 until 1999 Neptune is the "outermost planet."

Charon

Pluto's satellite

Pluto has **one known satellite**, Charon. It is 500 miles (800 km) across and is the only satellite apart from Earth's Moon that is not dwarfed by its planet.

Pluto

Planet X?

Astronomers used to think that Uranus and Neptune "wandered" in their orbits because they were pulled by the **gravity** of an unknown space body. They thought there might be another planet — **Planet X** — beyond Pluto. However, this now seems unlikely.

The Space Age began on October 4, 1957, when Russia launched the satellite **Sputnik 1**. This was a small metal sphere with four thin antennae. It contained a radio transmitter.

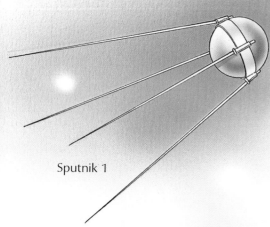

Sputnik 1

The development of **spacecraft** has moved incredibly quickly. **Probes**, **satellites**, **rockets,** and **space stations** have been successfully launched and have helped astronomers learn much more about the Solar System and beyond. Satellites also have many other uses for people on Earth.

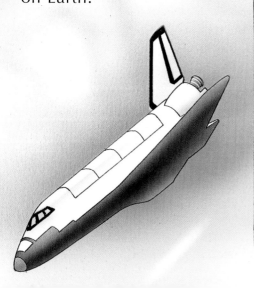

Getting off the ground

The invention of the **rocket** made Space exploration possible.

- As early as 1903, a Russian teacher called Tsiolkovskii suggested using liquid fuel for rockets and proposed rocket-building in separate parts, called stages.

V2

- Weapons called V2 rockets were developed by a German research team and used near the end of World War II. Space rockets were developed from them.

Vostock 1

Laika

- The Russians sent a small dog, called Laika, into orbit in Sputnik 2 in November 1957. She orbited Earth for a week and became the first living thing in space.

- In 1961, Yuri Gagarin, a Soviet cosmonaut, became the first person in space. He orbited Earth once in the spacecraft Vostock 1, landing safely after a 108-minute flight.

Space Shuttle

In 1981, the first **Space Shuttle**, *Columbia*, was launched in the U.S.A. For the first time a spacecraft could go into space and return to Earth, landing like a plane. It could then be used again for another flight.

1. The Shuttle plane, called an orbiter, is launched attached to a giant fuel tank and two solid-fuel boosters.

2. The boosters drop off at a height of 27 miles (43 km). They drop into the sea and are rescued for reuse.

3. At 71 miles (115 km) high, the fuel tank separates and burns up as it falls through Earth's atmosphere. It is the only part of the Shuttle that is not reused.

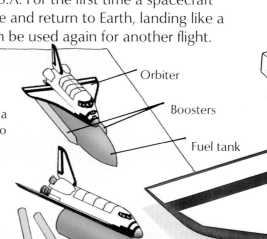

Orbiter

Boosters

Fuel tank

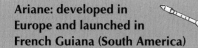
How do rockets work?

Rockets need a great deal of **power** to escape from Earth's gravity. Most have from two to four fuel-burning parts, called **stages**, that lift the rocket into orbit. The stages separate from the rocket as their fuel runs out. Then they burn up in the Earth's atmosphere.

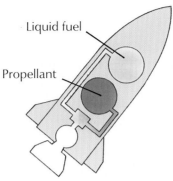

Liquid fuel

Propellant

1. Liquid-fuel rockets work by burning a mixture of fuel and a propellant.

2. The propellant makes the fuel catch fire with an explosive blast that pushes the rocket upward.

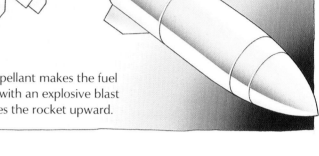

3. The rocket then builds up enormous speed — about three times faster than Concorde.

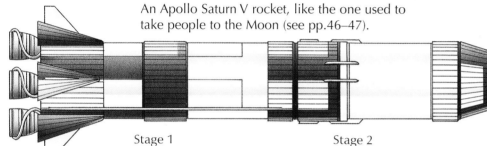

An Apollo Saturn V rocket, like the one used to take people to the Moon (see pp.46–47).

Stage 1

Stage 2

Stage 3

Capsule

Stage 1 separated from the rocket at a height of about 38 miles (61 km).

Stage 2 took the rocket up to about 114 miles (183 km).

Stage 3 took the Apollo capsule into Earth orbit and then to the Moon.

4. The Space Shuttle carries a large cargo. Once in space, the astronauts can repair or rescue satellites, launch new ones, or carry out experiments.

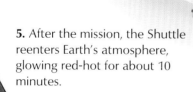

Satellite cargo

5. After the mission, the Shuttle reenters Earth's atmosphere, glowing red-hot for about 10 minutes.

6. It glides down to Earth and lands on a long runway, like an ordinary airplane.

Payload bay

• In 1986, the Space Shuttle *Challenger* exploded 73 seconds after blast-off. All seven astronauts were killed. It happened because of a tiny fault in one of the solid-fuel boosters.

Strange but true

• Yuri Gagarin survived the first manned spaceflight but was killed in a plane crash seven years later.

• Astronauts become a little taller in Space! There is less gravity, so their bones are less squashed together.

• As it comes back into Earth's atmosphere, the Space Shuttle reaches a temperature of 2,300°F (1,260°C).

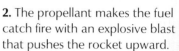

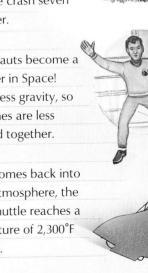

Landing on the Moon

This is some of the equipment used for experiments on the Moon:

Solar wind spectrometer measured the effect of solar wind

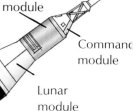

The Moon is the only place in the universe that people have **visited**. The effects of the journey on the astronauts, along with their experiments and rock samples, taught scientists a great deal about the Moon.

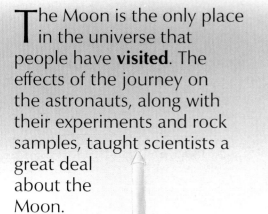

The **first Moon mission**, *Apollo II*, blasted off on July 16, 1969. The enormous Saturn 5 rocket carried the three American astronauts into space with the power of 160 jumbo jets. Four days later, Neil Armstrong stepped onto the Moon's surface and said the famous words: "That's one small step for a man, one giant leap for mankind."

The first Moon landing

Stacked at the top of the **Saturn 5 rocket** were the **Command Module**, the **Service Module**, and the **Lunar module**. Once in orbit around the Moon, the Lunar Module separated to start its journey to the Moon's surface.

- One astronaut, Michael Collins, stayed behind in the Command Module. Neil Armstrong and Edwin Aldrin were in the cramped Lunar Module.

Service module

Command module

Lunar module

The rocket as it was at takeoff.

The Lunar Module coming down to land on the Moon

- Minutes away from landing, Neil Armstrong took the controls, as the automatic navigation was taking them toward rocky ground. They landed safely on the Sea of Tranquillity.

Other Apollo missions

Six **Apollo missions** landed on the Moon between 1969 and 1972. Each one lasted longer than the last, and 842 pounds (382 kg) of Moon rock were collected for analysis.

- On the last three missions, the astronauts used a Moon buggy called the Lunar Rover.

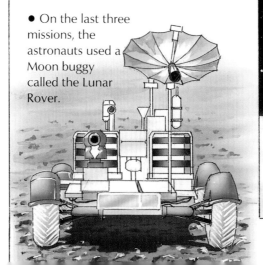

The Soviet missions

- In 1959, the Soviet unmanned probe, Luna 1, flew close to the Moon. A few months later Luna 2 landed on the Moon's surface. It was the first Earth-made object to land on another world.

- Soon after, Luna 3 flew past the far side of the Moon and took the first pictures of it.

- In 1966, Luna 9 landed on the Moon's surface and took the first close-up pictures of it.

Luna 9

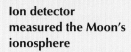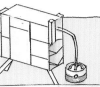
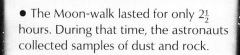

- The Moon-walk lasted for only 2½ hours. During that time, the astronauts collected samples of dust and rock.

- They also put up a U.S. flag, which they had to stiffen with wire as there is no wind on the Moon to blow it!

- The Moon has six times less gravity than Earth. This means that on the Moon astronauts weigh only a sixth of their normal weight. They could jump and spring about with ease, but it was difficult to walk.

- The astronauts tried to sleep in the Lunar Module, but it was much too cold. At night, temperatures reach −240°F (−150°C).

- The astronauts had to use special tools to collect rock samples, because they could not bend over in their spacesuits.

Moon discoveries

On Earth the surface is changing all the time. The Moon, however, is a dead place with **no atmosphere** and **no weather** to erode and change the landscape. So Moon dust and rock have lain in the same positions for millions of years. The youngest **Moon rock** analyzed was 3.1 billion years old.

Moon rock	Moonquake detector	The Moon
	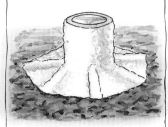	
• One sample of Moon rock was found to be about 4.6 billion years old — about the same age as Earth.	• Instruments detecting "moonquakes" found them to be much weaker than earthquakes.	• Because of the Apollo missions, the Moon has now been mapped more accurately than before.

Strange but true

- Astronauts' footprints and Lunar Rover tire tracks will stay on the Moon for millions of years as there is no wind to blow them away.

- The Moon is completely quiet, because there is no air to carry sound.

- Nothing can grow on the Moon, but plants did grow in Moon-soil on Earth.

Satellites

There are about 200 **artificial satellites** whirling around the Earth. There is also lots of junk in space, such as the remains of old satellites. Thousands have been launched and worked for a while before being replaced.

Satellites do all kinds of different jobs. Some can study Earth's **land** and **weather**, or beam **television pictures** and **telephone calls** across the world. Some can analyze **space radiation** that cannot penetrate the Earth's atmosphere. Some are used to **spy** on other countries.

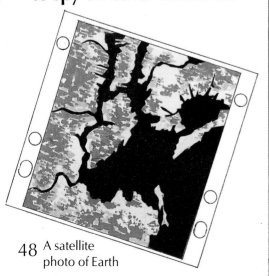

48 A satellite photo of Earth

Getting into orbit

Satellites are taken into space by **rockets** or by **Space Shuttle**. They are carried in the Shuttle's cargo, or payload, bay and then launched into orbit in Space.

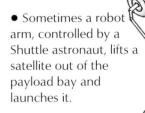

- Sometimes a robot arm, controlled by a Shuttle astronaut, lifts a satellite out of the payload bay and launches it.

- These are some of the kinds of orbit a satellite might use:

- Most satellites have their own rocket launchers that boost them into orbit when they are at a safe distance from the Shuttle.

- Geostationary orbit: the satellite orbits at the same speed as Earth's spin. It is always above the same point on Earth, at a height of about 22,000 miles (36,000 km).

- Polar orbit: the satellite orbits Earth from north to south, and can cover most of the Earth within a day. This orbit is usually at a height of about 620 miles (1,000 km).

- Eccentric orbit: the satellite flies low over parts of the Earth before swinging out to complete the orbit.

Different kinds of satellites

Communications satellites (comsats) beam telephone calls and television pictures from one part of the world to another. They receive a picture from Earth and send it on to its destination.

Intelsat 6

A Molniya satellite

- In 1965, Russian Molniya satellites began the world's biggest network of comsats.

- Intelsat 6 carries 120,000 telephone circuits and three television channels.

Power from Space

Satellites have large **solar panels** to trap energy from the Sun.

- Satellites store the Sun's energy in batteries and use it to power their equipment.

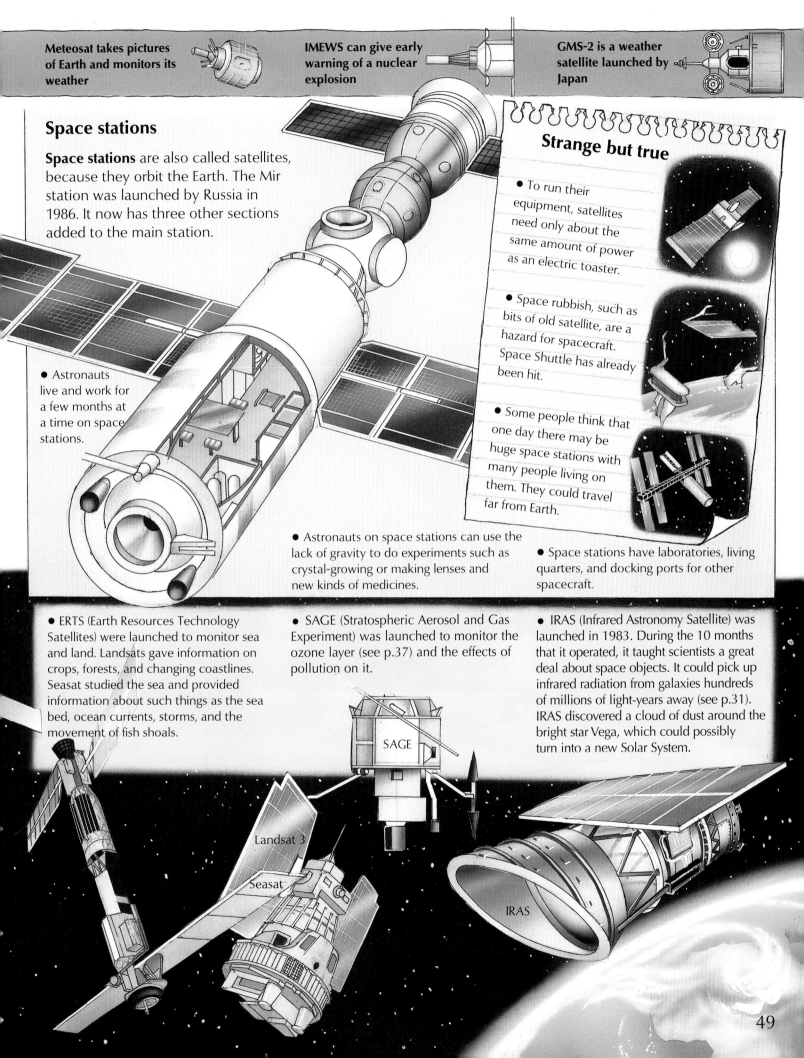

Space stations

Space stations are also called satellites, because they orbit the Earth. The Mir station was launched by Russia in 1986. It now has three other sections added to the main station.

• Astronauts live and work for a few months at a time on space stations.

Strange but true

• To run their equipment, satellites need only about the same amount of power as an electric toaster.

• Space rubbish, such as bits of old satellite, are a hazard for spacecraft. Space Shuttle has already been hit.

• Some people think that one day there may be huge space stations with many people living on them. They could travel far from Earth.

• Astronauts on space stations can use the lack of gravity to do experiments such as crystal-growing or making lenses and new kinds of medicines.

• Space stations have laboratories, living quarters, and docking ports for other spacecraft.

• ERTS (Earth Resources Technology Satellites) were launched to monitor sea and land. Landsats gave information on crops, forests, and changing coastlines. Seasat studied the sea and provided information about such things as the sea bed, ocean currents, storms, and the movement of fish shoals.

• SAGE (Stratospheric Aerosol and Gas Experiment) was launched to monitor the ozone layer (see p.37) and the effects of pollution on it.

• IRAS (Infrared Astronomy Satellite) was launched in 1983. During the 10 months that it operated, it taught scientists a great deal about space objects. It could pick up infrared radiation from galaxies hundreds of millions of light-years away (see p.31). IRAS discovered a cloud of dust around the bright star Vega, which could possibly turn into a new Solar System.

SAGE

Landsat 3

Seasat

IRAS

49

The First People

Pebble tools: Homo habilis (2.5 million years ago)

The first recognizable **human beings** probably appeared about 2 million years ago, although groups of human-like creatures existed before then. People looking similar to ourselves have lived on Earth for only about 100,000 years — which is just a fraction of time in the history of the Earth.

The first humans

Scientists studying **fossils** of bones and other remains have managed to piece together some idea of what the **first humans** were like.

Australopithecines

Homo Habilis

● About 3.5 million years ago, Australopithecines lived in Africa. They had apelike faces but walked upright and probably used sticks and pieces of bone as tools.

● About 2 million years ago, creatures called Homo Habilis (handy man) lived in Africa. They had larger brains than Australopithecines. They sharpened stones to make tools, built shelters, and worked together to hunt animals.

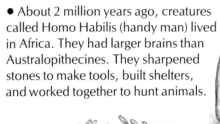

Neanderthal skull

Modern skull

Homo Erectus

● About 1.6 million years ago Homo Erectus (upright man) appeared, first in Africa then also spreading to Asia. These people were taller than Homo Habilis, with larger brains. They used many different stone tools and discovered how to use fire for cooking and keeping warm.

A Neanderthal man

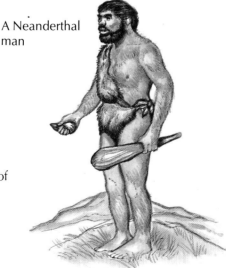

● About 200,000 to 100,000 years ago, Homo Sapiens (thinking man) appeared. People today belong to this group. The Neanderthal people were an early kind of Homo Sapiens. They lived in caves in Europe 60,000 years ago, wore animal skins, and made carvings of animals.

Strange but true

● The axes in use today are very like some of the earliest hunting weapons.

● About 1 million years ago, some humans built huts from mammoth bones covered over with animal skins.

● Early humans may have learned to cook meat by accidentally dropping it onto a fire.

● The human being's nearest animal relatives are thought to be gorillas, chimpanzees, and orangutans.

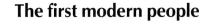

The first modern people

The Neanderthal people gradually died out, but by this time other types of **Homo Sapiens** had developed and spread around the world. These are some of the things the **first modern humans** did:

● Decorated tools with pictures of animals and painted hunting scenes on the walls of their cave homes.

● Made jewelry from shells and animal teeth, and clothes from skins sewn together with needles made of bone.

● Buried their dead, painting the bodies red and putting tools and weapons in the graves. This may have been part of a religious ceremony, showing belief in life after death.

The first farmers

At first, people lived as **nomads**, which means they wandered around in small groups or tribes searching for good hunting grounds. About 10,000 years ago an important change took place. People living in the Middle East began to settle down and farm. These **first farmers** learned how to:

● Sow seeds and grow crops.

● Capture wild goats and sheep and breed them to provide people with milk, meat, and skins.

● Build houses of mud and straw that dried hard in the sun.

● Bake bread in ovens. Early bread was flat and hard.

Towns and trading

When people settled in groups or communities, they sometimes produced more goods than they needed for themselves. So they began to **trade** their extra goods for other things made by people nearby. Gradually, towns grew in size and became busy **trading centers**.

● People living in settled farming communities had more time to develop skills such as pottery, weaving, and toolmaking.

● Eventually, some people became craftworkers, specializing in making certain goods to sell.

● Before money was invented, people bartered (exchanged) their goods. People with spare wheat, for example, might swap it with someone else for pottery or wool.

Weaving at a loom

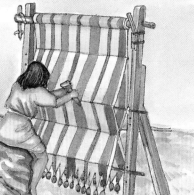

People of the World

For thousands of years the **number of people** living on Earth increased very slowly. Early peoples lived **shorter lives** than most people do today. Very little was known about **medicine**, so many people died from illness or injury before they reached old age.

Today, in many countries people are better housed and fed and there are **medical services** to take care of illness, so people live longer. As a result, the number of people in the world has grown rapidly.

B.C. and A.D.

The letters B.C. after a number mean the years before the birth of Christ. A.D. stands for the Latin words *anno domini* (year of Our Lord) and means a date after the birth of Christ.

● B.C. numbers count backward, so (for example) 1000 B.C. is further back in time than 500 B.C.

How cities have grown

These are the populations of some of the world's largest **cities**, now and in the past:

The population explosion

About 155 people are born every minute of every day. This recent rise in population is often called the **population explosion**. If this rate of growth continues, the world population will have tripled by the end of the next century.

● World population grew much more slowly in the past. It took about 11,500 years for it to grow from 10 million to 500 million. Since 1800 it has grown very quickly.

This diagram shows how the population has increased over the last thousand years.

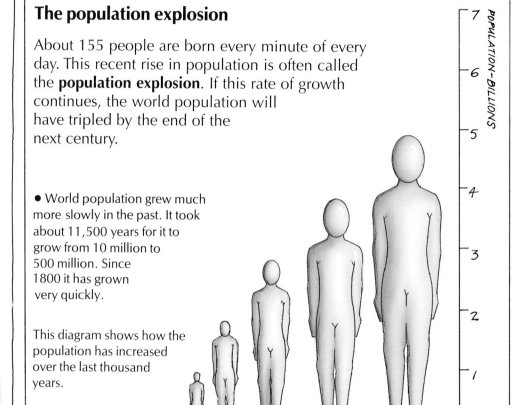

These are some **population figures** from the past:

● In 8000 B.C. there were probably only about 6 million people in the world. Most lived in Asia and Africa.

● By A.D. 1, people had spread to most parts of the world. The population had grown to about 255 million.

● By 1600 the world population had doubled to about 500 million.

● In 1987 the world population rose to 5 billion, ten times as many people as in 1600. About three-fourths of the world's people today live in Asia and Europe.

● At its present rate of growth, the world population doubles about every 40 years.

● 27,000 B.C.: The city of Dolní Vestonice (in modern Czechoslovakia) contained about 100 people

Jericho

● 7800 B.C.: Jericho (now in occupied Jordan) contained about 27,000 people

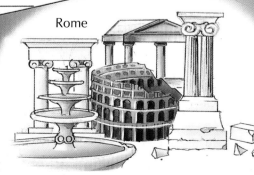

Rome

● As early as 133 B.C., Rome was a huge city with a million inhabitants

Great Britain:
75 years

U.S.A.:
76 years

Ethiopia:
52 years

Strange but true

- The Chinese population is increasing at 35,000 a day — over 12 million a year!

- At present, one person in three is under 15 years of age. Fewer than one person in ten is over 64 years of age.

- It is estimated that the average length of life in A.D. 400 was about 33 years for a man and 27 for a woman.

- In these countries most people live in towns or cities: UK 91%, Australia 85%, U.S.A. and Japan 76%. In these countries, most people live and work in farming: India 72%, Kenya 80%, and Burkino Faso (Africa) 91%.

Population problems

The rapid rise in population has created many **problems**:

- Shortage of food. To feed everyone, we will have to produce more food and share it out more fairly.

- Pollution due to the increased use of fuels. Supplies of oil, coal, and gas are also running low and cannot be replaced.

- Destruction of wildlife habitats for housing, industry, and farming.

- Widespread poverty and hunger, especially in Africa and Asia.

- Shortage of housing.

- Unemployment.

Countries

At present, the world is divided into about 170 **independent countries**. This number keeps changing, as countries join together or become separate.

- An independent country is one that has its own government, makes its own laws, and has its own flag.

Vatican City

- The smallest independent country in the world is Vatican City in Rome. It has an area of 109 acres (0.4 sq-km) governed by the Roman Catholic Church.

- The country with the highest population is China, with over 1 billion people living there.

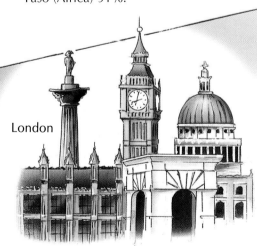

London

- London did not have one million inhabitants until 1800. Now it has over 6 million

Tokyo

- Some modern cities:
Mexico City, 17 million
Tokyo, Japan, 27 million
New York, 17.5 million
Shanghai, China, 13.5 million

The **human body** is made up of many different parts, including billions of **cells**, thousands of miles of **tubing**, and hundreds of **muscles** and **bones**. Each of the many different parts of the body has its own special job, but all the parts have to work together to keep the body alive.

Cells

Everything in the body is made up of tiny living units called **cells**. A fully grown body has about **50 billion cells**.

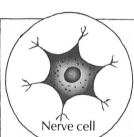

Nerve cell

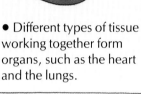

Heart

- A group of similar cells doing the same job is called tissue. Muscles and nerves are tissues.

- Different types of tissue working together form organs, such as the heart and the lungs.

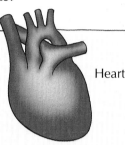

Heart position

The skeleton

The **skeleton** is a framework, made of about **206 bones**, that supports the body, gives it shape, and protects it from damage.

- The skull protects the brain and the ribs protect the heart.

- Joints are where two bones meet. Some are fixed but others can bend.

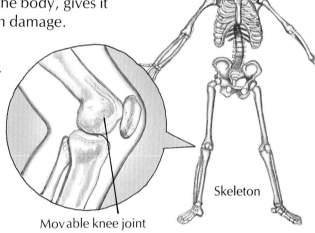

Movable knee joint

Skeleton

Muscles

The human body has about **650 muscles**. They enable the skeleton to **move**.

- Muscles move by contracting (tensing) or relaxing (loosening). They are joined to bones by fibers. When muscles contract, the fibers pull the bones and make them move. Most muscles work in pairs, pulling opposite ways.

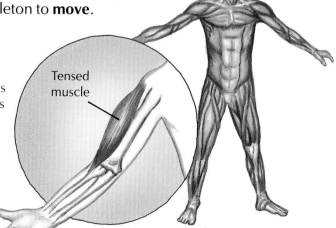

Body muscles

Tensed muscle

Strange but true

- The hair on your head usually lives for 2 to 6 years before dropping out. Eyelash hairs last for only about 10 weeks.

- Most people have 12 pairs of rib bones, but some have 13.

- On average, a human being eats 50 tons of food and drinks 13,000 gallons (50,000 liters) of liquid in a lifetime.

- Each person walks about 15,000 miles (25,000 km) during a lifetime.

The blood system

Blood carries **oxygen gas** and dissolved food particles called **nutrients** to all the cells in the body, so that they can make **energy**.

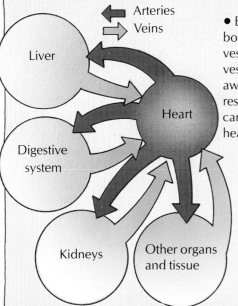

→ Arteries
⇨ Veins

Liver

Heart

Digestive system

Kidneys

Other organs and tissue

• Blood flows around the body in tubes called vessels. Arteries are blood vessels that carry blood away from the heart to the rest of the body. Veins carry blood back to the heart.

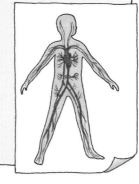

The lungs

Oxygen passes into the blood through the lung walls when we breathe in. Waste **carbon dioxide** gas is passed back into the lungs from the blood.

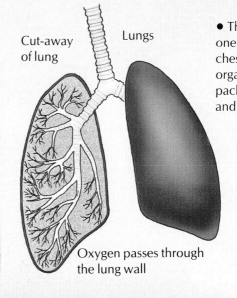

Cut-away of lung

Lungs

Oxygen passes through the lung wall

• There are two lungs, one in each side of the chest. They are spongy organs made of tightly packed tissue, nerves, and blood vessels.

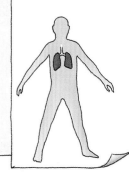

The digestive system

Everything a human being eats has to be broken down by the body before **nutrients** from the food can be taken into the blood and turned into energy.

This process takes place in the **digestive system**, a series of connected parts that make up a passage beginning at the mouth and ending at the anus.

1. Food goes down the throat into the stomach, where chemicals called digestive juices break it down.

2. The food passes on to the small intestine (about 20 feet (6m) long), where most digestion takes place.

3. Nutrients pass through the intestine wall. They are carried by the blood to the liver, which stores them or sends them where they are needed.

4. The food goes into the large intestine. If there is any water or other useful substance left, they pass into the blood through the intestine wall.

5. The kidneys filter out liquid waste called urine. It is stored in the bladder until you go to the toilet.

6. Solid waste is stored in the rectum at the end of the intestine. It leaves your body through the anus as feces.

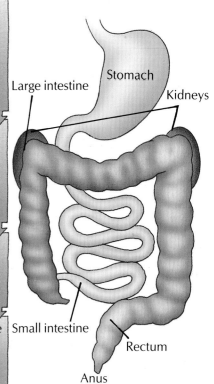

Large intestine

Stomach

Kidneys

Small intestine

Rectum

Anus

Body Controls

The human body has a very efficient system for **sensing** the world around it. It can feel, see, hear, smell, and taste things and deal with all this information better than any computer. It has to do this to survive.

All the information the body receives is processed by the **brain**, which is more highly developed in humans than in any other animal species.

Brain power

The **brain** is the body's **control center**. It keeps the body running smoothly, thinks and makes decisions, stores memories, and produces feelings such as happiness, anger, and sorrow.

- The body is continually sending messages to the brain telling it what is happening. The brain sends messages back telling the body parts what to do. The messages pass along nerves that run throughout the body.

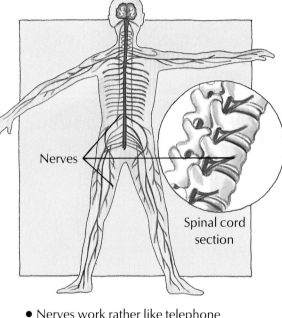

Nerves

Spinal cord section

- Nerves work rather like telephone wires, carrying information in the form of tiny electrical signals.

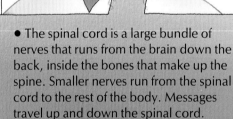
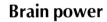

- The spinal cord is a large bundle of nerves that runs from the brain down the back, inside the bones that make up the spine. Smaller nerves run from the spinal cord to the rest of the body. Messages travel up and down the spinal cord.

- The brain gets messages about the world outside the body from the senses. People have five main senses — sight, hearing, smell, taste, and touch. The sense organs are the body parts that sense things. They are the eyes, ears, nose, tongue, and skin.

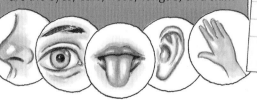

Strange but true

- An adult's brain weighs about 3 pounds (1.4 kg). It is roughly the shape of a cauliflower.

- The body's fastest messages pass along the nerves at 250 mph (400km/h).

- Very few women are color-blind, but on average 1 in 12 men cannot see some colors properly.

- One brain cell may be connected to as many as 25,000 other brain cells.

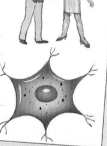

Seeing

The **eye** has a special lining called the **retina**. This contains cells that are sensitive to light. Messages from these cells pass along **nerves** to the **brain**, which works out what the eyes are looking at.

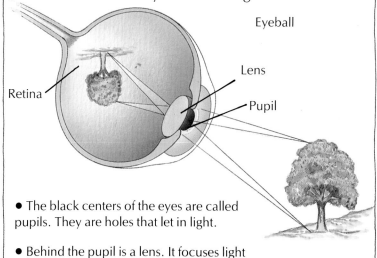

Eyeball

Lens

Retina

Pupil

- The black centers of the eyes are called pupils. They are holes that let in light.

- Behind the pupil is a lens. It focuses light rays into an upside-down picture on the retina inside the back of the eyeball. The brain turns the image the right way up.

Hearing

The part of the ear you can see is called the **outer ear**. This collects and funnels sounds into the **inner ear**. Inside the inner ear:

- The sounds make the eardrum vibrate, or shake. The vibrations pass on through two small bones called the hammer and the anvil, and then through a group of three tiny bones called the stirrup.

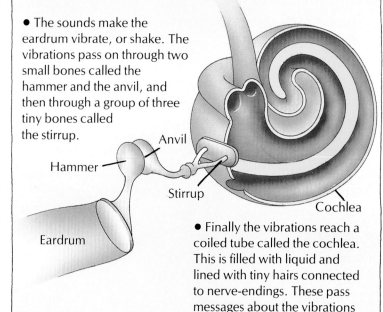

Anvil

Hammer

Stirrup

Cochlea

Eardrum

- Finally the vibrations reach a coiled tube called the cochlea. This is filled with liquid and lined with tiny hairs connected to nerve-endings. These pass messages about the vibrations to the brain.

Smelling and tasting

Inside the back of the **nose** there are nerve-endings that pick up **smells** and send messages about them to the brain. On the **tongue**, special groups of cells called **tastebuds** pick up and send messages about **taste**.

- Tiny smell molecules travel through the air and enter the nasal cavity behind your nose.

Nasal cavity

Magnified tastebud

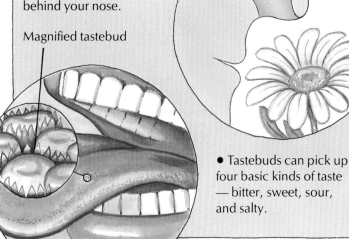

- Tastebuds can pick up four basic kinds of taste — bitter, sweet, sour, and salty.

Touching

Your **skin** is full of nerve-endings that supply the brain with information about **touch**. There are lots of different nerve-endings to pick up information about different kinds of touch sensations.

- A piece of skin the size of a small coin has at least 35 nerve-endings in it, as well as over 3 million cells, 3 feet (1m) of blood vessels, and many tiny bundles of cells called glands, which produce sweat and oil.

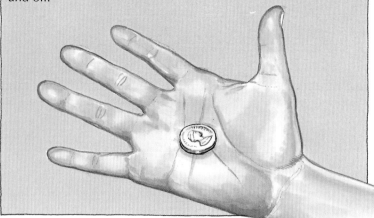

57

New Life

All new life begins with just one **cell**. To make this first cell, a male **sperm** must enter a female **egg** called an **ovum**. The cell then starts growing and dividing to make new cells. These divide in turn to make the millions of cells found in the human body. The creation of new life is called **reproduction**.

People grow and change throughout their lives, from birth to old age. No two human beings are exactly the same in looks or in personality, but everyone goes through the same stages of development.

How babies are born

The moment when a sperm enters an egg is called **conception** or **fertilization**.

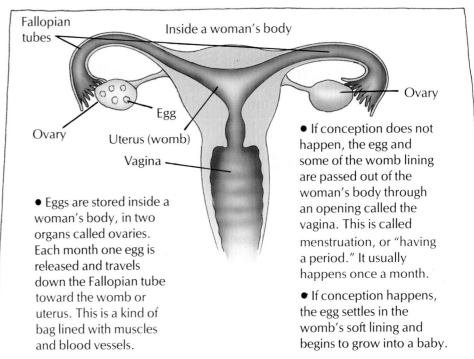

Fallopian tubes

Inside a woman's body

Egg

Ovary

Ovary

Uterus (womb)

Vagina

● Eggs are stored inside a woman's body, in two organs called ovaries. Each month one egg is released and travels down the Fallopian tube toward the womb or uterus. This is a kind of bag lined with muscles and blood vessels.

● If conception does not happen, the egg and some of the womb lining are passed out of the woman's body through an opening called the vagina. This is called menstruation, or "having a period." It usually happens once a month.

● If conception happens, the egg settles in the womb's soft lining and begins to grow into a baby.

Strange but true

● Children tend to grow faster in spring and summer.

● On average, women tend to live longer than men.

● If you carried on growing as fast as a baby does in the womb, you would be 50 feet (15m) by the time your were 10 years old!

● The most babies born to a mother at one birth is 10.

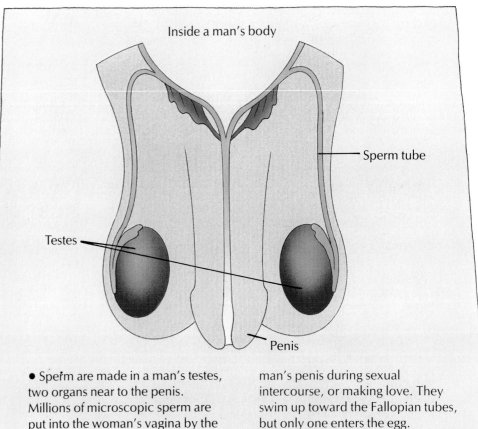

Inside a man's body

Sperm tube

Testes

Penis

● Sperm are made in a man's testes, two organs near to the penis. Millions of microscopic sperm are put into the woman's vagina by the

man's penis during sexual intercourse, or making love. They swim up toward the Fallopian tubes, but only one enters the egg.

58

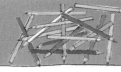
Iron: as much as in a 1 inch (2.5 cm-long) nail

Carbon: as much as in 9,000 pencils

Water: two-thirds of the body is water. Adults contain about 12 gallons (45l).

How babies grow

From **conception** to **birth** takes about 38 weeks. Here are some of the stages along the way:

● Six weeks: the baby is very small, about an inch (2.4 cm) long. It has begun to develop a nervous system, a heart, a digestive tract, and sense organs. It has buds that will develop into arms and legs.

● Twelve weeks: the baby is between 2½ and 3 inches (6.25 cm and 7.5 cm) long. It is inside a fluid-filled bag called the amniotic sac, connected to its mother by an umbilical cord.

● Twenty-eight weeks: the baby is between 12 and 14 inches (30 and 36 cm) long and weighs about 30 ounces (900 grams.) A creamy-colored wax has now developed over its body.

● Around 38 weeks: the baby is ready to be born. It is 20 inches (50 cm) long and weighs 6 to 11 pounds (3 to 5 kg).

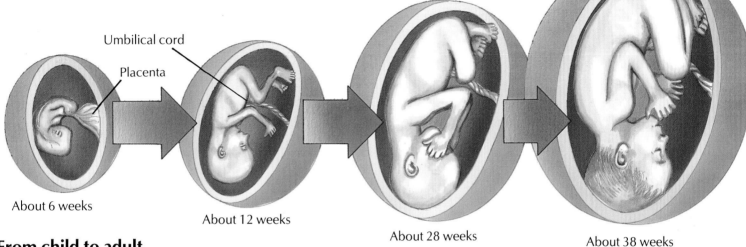

Umbilical cord

Placenta

About 6 weeks

About 12 weeks

About 28 weeks

About 38 weeks

From child to adult

The period of time when children are growing into adults is called **adolescence**. The early part of adolescence, when bodies change, is called **puberty**. The changes take place at any time between the ages of 10 and 15. Here are some of them:

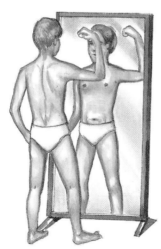

● Girls start to menstruate (have periods). Their breasts start to grow bigger, their hips get broader and they grow more body hair.

● Boys start making sperm in their testes. They grow facial hair and their voices "break" or deepen. Their shoulders and chests get broader.

Growing older

Once people are fully grown their bodies very slowly start to **wear out** and **slow down**.

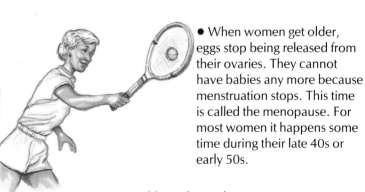

● When women get older, eggs stop being released from their ovaries. They cannot have babies any more because menstruation stops. This time is called the menopause. For most women it happens some time during their late 40s or early 50s.

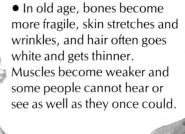

● In old age, bones become more fragile, skin stretches and wrinkles, and hair often goes white and gets thinner. Muscles become weaker and some people cannot hear or see as well as they once could.

Although many creatures communicate with each other using sounds, only humans have developed **spoken language** to tell each other about their ideas and feelings.

There are about 5,000 languages in the world today, but many of them are spoken only by small groups of people. Most languages have variations or **dialects** – different forms of a language that are spoken only in particular areas.

People have tried to invent a new language that everyone in the world could share. The most successful so far is **Esperanto**, which more than 100 million people have learned since its invention in 1887.

Learning a language

Most young children learn the **language** spoken by their **family** very easily, almost without knowing they are doing so.

● Babies learn by listening to the voices they hear around them and by copying sounds and words.

● By the time they are two years old, most children can use several hundred words.

● Children who are brought up hearing two languages all the time soon learn to speak both. Someone who speaks two languages is called bilingual.

Languages

Languages are divided into groups, called **families**. All the languages in a family developed from one earlier language.

● About 48% (almost half the world's people) speak a language from the Indo-European family. This includes all the major languages of Europe as well as some from Iran and India.

● About 23% (nearly a quarter of the world's people) speak one of the Chinese family of languages.

mat (Russian)
meter (Greek)
madre (Spanish)
mutter (Germany)
mère (French)
mother (English)

● Here are some words for "mother" in Indo-European languages. They all come from the word *mata*, which is "mother" in the ancient Sanskrit language.

Changing languages

Languages change all the time. Words may be **borrowed** from other languages, or **invented** to name a new idea or object.

● Many English words have been invented. For example, the word *television* was invented using *tele* (a Greek word meaning "far") and *vision* (from the Latin word for "to see").

● These English words were borrowed: *Mosquito* (Spanish), *Tea* (Chinese), *Sugar* (Arabic), *Shampoo* (Hindi), *Ski* (Norwegian), *Robot* (Czech), *Ketchup* (Malay), *Parka* (Russian).

Writing things down

Writing developed much later than spoken language. Here are some facts about **written languages**:

Hieroglyph examples

 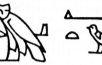

Greek alphabet

αβγδεζηθικλμνξοπρσςτυφφχψω
ΑΒΓΔΕΖΗΘΙΚΛΜΝΞΟΠΡΣΤΥΦ
ΧΨΩ 1234567890 .,:;

Arabic alphabet

ابتثجحخدذر زسشصضطظعغفقكلمنهوىلا
١٢٣٤٥٦٧٨٩٠

Chinese symbols

拿 生
個 火
燈 你

- The first written languages used picture symbols to represent whole words.

- The earliest-known picture symbols were used in the Iranian region in about 3500 B.C. The Ancient Egyptians began using picture symbols called hieroglyphics in about 3000 B.C.

- Most modern languages are written in alphabets. The words are spelled out with letters. Each letter represents a sound.

- The Phoenicians, who lived along the Mediterranean, developed the first alphabet in about 1000 B.C.

- Chinese is the only major modern language that has no alphabet. Instead it has around 50,000 picture symbols.

- Some Chinese words are made from one symbol. Others are made up of various symbols mixed together.

Speaking without words

Movements made by the face, head, arms, hands, and body can signal thoughts and feelings almost as clearly as spoken words. These signals are called **body language**.

- When people are nervous they often fidget with their hands.

- The distance between people who are talking to each other is important. If one person stands too close, the other one may feel threatened and move away.

- Body language varies from place to place. For example, in some countries looking a person straight in the eye means that you are honest and truthful. In other countries it is regarded as bad manners.

Strange but true

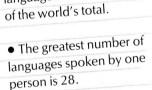

- O is the oldest letter in our alphabet. It has not changed since 1300 B.C. **O**

- The small country of Papua New Guinea has about 500 separate languages – about 10% of the world's total.

- The greatest number of languages spoken by one person is 28.

- The most complicated written character in Chinese is made up of 64 brushstrokes and means 'talkative'!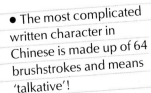

61

Food

Without food, people cannot survive. Food gives the body **energy** to make it work.

To stay healthy, you need a **balanced diet**: a good mixture of the different kinds of food available. Sadly, many people in the world today do not have enough food to eat.

Meal with animal products

Vegetarian meal

All food comes from plants or animals. Humans are **omnivorous**, which means they are able to eat both meat and plants. However, some people choose to be **vegetarian**, which means they do not eat meat.

Plant food

Plants that grow well in a particular part of the world provide the **staple diet**, or main food, of that area. Here are some staple foods and the places where they are eaten:

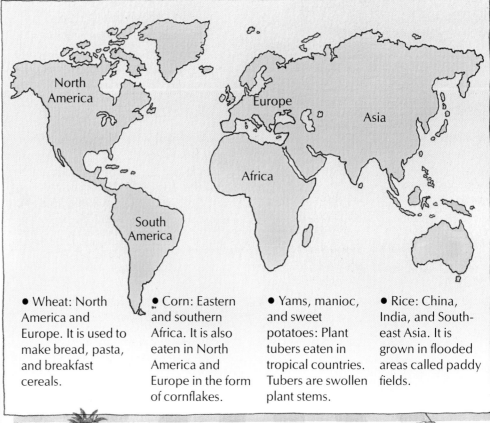

- Wheat: North America and Europe. It is used to make bread, pasta, and breakfast cereals.

- Corn: Eastern and southern Africa. It is also eaten in North America and Europe in the form of cornflakes.

- Yams, manioc, and sweet potatoes: Plant tubers eaten in tropical countries. Tubers are swollen plant stems.

- Rice: China, India, and Southeast Asia. It is grown in flooded areas called paddy fields.

Fruits and vegetables

These **plant foods** help to make a healthy diet:

- Fruit contains a plant's seeds. Many fruits are sweet and juicy.

- Vegetables come from different plant parts. Here are some examples:

ROOTS: carrots, beets, and parsnips

LEAVES: lettuce and spinach

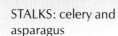

STALKS: celery and asparagus

BUDS: cabbage and brussels sprouts

SEEDS: peas, beans, and sweet corn

FLOWERS: cauliflower

What food contains

Food contains **nutrients**, which the body needs to keep it healthy. Here are the main nutrients, what they do, and a list of some of the foods in which they are found:

Nutrients	What They Do	Where Found
Proteins	Help the body cells to grow and repair injuries	Meat, fish, cheese, eggs, beans
Carbohydrates	Provide energy	Bread, potatoes, pasta, rice, flour, sugar
Fats	Build body cells and provide energy	Milk, cheese, oils, butter, oily fish, nuts
Vitamins	Keep the body healthy	There are about 20 vitamins, found in many different foods. Vitamin C, for example, is found in fruit and vegetables
Minerals	Many minerals are found in food, including calcium (builds teeth and bone) and iron (keeps blood healthy)	Cheese, milk (calcium) Liver, brown bread (iron)

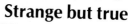

Cooking food

The first humans ate their food raw. Then, about 500,000 years ago, people learned how to use fire for **cooking**. This is what cooking does:

• Breaks down tough food so that you can eat and digest it more easily. Cooking different foods together creates new tastes.

• Helps to preserve food from going rotten. It also destroys some nutrients, so vegetables and fruit are sometimes better for you if eaten raw.

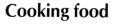

Homes

People need **homes** where they can eat, sleep, and shelter from the weather. Most houses are made of materials that are easy to find in the place where they are built. They are usually designed to suit the **climate** of their area.

In some countries people build their own homes. In other countries, architects design houses and builders construct them.

Shapes and sizes

Here are some traditional house styles from around the world, built to suit the **climate** and local **materials**.

- Iceland: turf roofs are used to keep the heat in.

- Arctic: Inuit (Eskimo) people build temporary houses made of blocks of snow, called igloos.

Homes on the move

Nomads are people who have no fixed home. They move around looking for work or pastures for their animals.

Strange but true

- The world's largest palace has 1,788 rooms. It was built for the Sultan of Brunei.

- Toilets were not installed in most houses until the mid 1800s.

- The world's tallest apartment house is the Metropolitan Tower in New York. People live in the top 48 stories, with 30 office floors below.

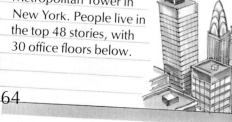

Middle East:
cave
dwellings

Hong Kong:
houseboat on
the harbor

California:
experimental
house run on solar
power

• South America: the Queche Indians build homes of mud bricks with thick pampas grass on the roof.

• Around the Mediterranean: many houses are painted white to reflect sunshine. Some have window shutters to keep the inside cool.

• Switzerland: houses have long sloping roofs so that snow can slide off them in winter.

• Asia: in marshy areas, people live in houses built on stilts to protect them from floods and wild animals.

• Big cities: land is scarce and expensive so buildings are built high into the air with lots of families living in each building.

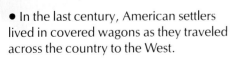

• In the last century, American settlers lived in covered wagons as they traveled across the country to the West.

• In the Sahara Desert nomadic people live in tents made from cloth of woven goat hair. The sides can be rolled up to let cool breezes in.

• In Iran the Turkoman people live in circular tents made of wood and felt.

• In Siberia some nomadic people live in tents made of walrus skin.

Houses in the past

Here are some **ancient** house styles:

Roman villa

Dugout hut

• Prehistoric dugout hut (Europe: about 3000 B.C.).

• Roman villa built around a courtyard (Europe: about 2,000 years ago).

• Half-timbered houses (parts of Northern Europe: 500 years ago).

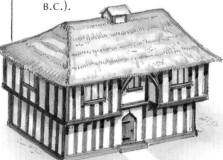

Half-timbered houses

Religion

Religions are beliefs that are found all over the world. They have **rules of behavior** that their followers obey, and a **god** or **gods** that they worship. There are usually special **religious ceremonies** and **places of worship**.

Religion began thousands of years ago. Early humans explained natural events such as thunderstorms by saying that gods made them happen. People also made gods of the Sun, Moon, and Earth. They prayed to them for good hunting or crops.

Today, millions of people follow one or other of the major world religions.

World religions

These are the major **world religions**:

● Christianity: founded by Jesus Christ, whose birth nearly 2,000 years ago marks the beginning of the Christian calendar. Christians believe there is one God, and that Jesus Christ was God on Earth in human form. Their holy book is the Bible.

● Hinduism: developed in India at least 2,500 years ago. There are many gods, with Brahma as the most important. Hindus believe in reincarnation, which means that people are reborn many times. In each new life they are rewarded or punished for their deeds in an earlier life.

● Shinto: a Japanese religion whose followers believe that spirits are present in all living things. They worship at holy places called shrines.

An Anglican (Christian) bishop

Strange but true

● Archaeologists think that some caves in Europe were used as places of worship more than 14,000 years ago.

● The world's largest temple is Angkor Wat in Cambodia. It is over 1,000 years old.

● The largest recorded gathering of people was at a Hindu religious festival in India in 1989. It was attended by about 15 million people.

Holy objects

In all religions, **holy places** and **sacred objects** are an important part of worship.

● Copies of the Torah, the Jewish Holy Law, are written in Hebrew on parchment scrolls and kept in a casket called the Ark.

Jewish religious service

St. Peter's

● St. Peter's in Vatican City was until recently the world's largest Christian church. The largest church is now in the Ivory Coast, Africa. It was completed in 1989.

A Buddhist priest

• Buddhism: founded in India about 2,500 years ago by Siddhartha Gautama, who was given the title "Buddha." He said that people could escape suffering and find perfect peace ("nirvana") by following his teachings.

• Islam: the religion of Muslims – people who follow the teaching of Muhammad. It was founded nearly 1,400 years ago in the Middle East when the prophet Muhammad received messages from Allah (God). They were written down to form the Koran, the Islamic sacred book.

• Judaism: the religion of Jewish people, founded more than 4,000 years ago. Jews believe in one God who has chosen them to pass on his Commandments (laws) to the world. They believe a Messiah (savior) will come from God to bring peace to the world.

Odin

Ancient religions

• The Viking people of Scandinavia had many gods. The most important, Odin, rode an eight-legged horse. The gods lived in a paradise called Valhalla.

• Aztec people, who lived in Mexico about 800 years ago, worshiped many gods. They made human sacrifices by killing people and tearing out their hearts.

The Ka'bah in Mecca

• The Ka'bah in Mecca, Saudi Arabia, contains a sacred black stone. It is the most holy shrine of Islam. Many thousands of Muslims visit it each year.

• Statues of the Buddha decorate Buddhist temples and shrines.

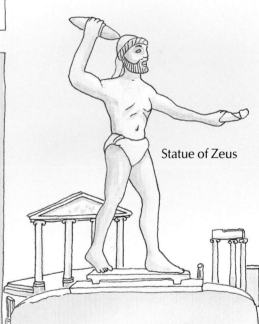

Statue of Zeus

• The Ancient Greeks believed in many gods and goddesses, who lived on Mount Olympus. Zeus was the chief god.

• Ancestor worship still survives in parts of Africa and China. People believe the dead look after the living, so they perform ceremonies to their ancestors in the hope they will bring good luck.

Government

To live together in peace, people need to agree on certain rules or **laws**. Each country of the world has a **government** that makes decisions about how a country should be run, and makes the laws for its people. The kind of government varies from one country to another.

Governments collect **taxes**, which is money taken from the wages that people earn. These taxes are used to pay for such things as schools, hospitals, and roads.

Democracy

Most Western countries are **democracies**. Democracy means:.

- "Rule by the people." People vote to choose representatives who take part in the government of the country.

- There is a choice of political parties to elect (vote for).

- There are basic human rights, such as the freedom to criticize the government.

Communism

There have been **communist** governments in Russia, China, Cuba, and parts of Africa. There are few communist countries left. Under communism:

- People can vote, but only for officials of the Communist Party.

- All factories, farms, and stores are owned by the state.

- There is no freedom of speech; no one is allowed to criticize the government or its leaders.

Dictatorship

In a **dictatorship**, one person holds all the power. The people are not allowed to take any part in government or to criticize the leader.

- The Ancient Romans sometimes passed all power to one man — a dictator — in times of war. This ensured that they had a strong leader in a time of trouble. After the war, his power was supposed to end.

- Modern dictators have included Hitler (Germany), Stalin (USSR), Mao Tse-tung (China), Ceausescu (Romania), and Saddam Hussein (Iraq).

Strange but true

- English medieval monks practiced a form of communal government. They owned all their possessions jointly.

- New Zealand was the first country to allow women to vote. This happened in 1893.

- The world's largest election was held in India in 1989. Over 304 million people voted and 3½ million staff were needed to collect the votes.

68

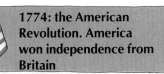

1774: the American Revolution. America won independence from Britain

1789: the French Revolution. The king was overthrown and a republic set up

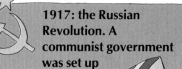

1917: the Russian Revolution. A communist government was set up

Government by parliament

The word **parliament** comes from an old French word meaning "to talk." Parliament is where politicians elected by the people meet to discuss problems and govern the country. The **British parliamentary system** is the oldest in the world:

- The British parliament is divided into the House of Commons and the House of Lords. Members of the House of Lords are not elected.

- King Edward I of England held a parliament in 1295. All later parliaments are based on it.

- Many other countries have parliaments based on the British system.

Houses of Parliament, London

- In Britain the monarch (king or queen) heads the country but is not directly involved in government. Monarchs inherit their titles and are not elected.

Government of the U.S.A.

The United States of America is a **republic** (a country without a king or queen). It is led by an elected **president**.

- Each state has its own local government. The national government in Washington controls all the state governments.

The White House, Washington, D.C., home of the President.

- People vote in elections for the political party they want to govern the country. The leader of the winning party becomes the president.

- There are three branches of government: the Executive, Congress, and the Supreme Court. In this way, power is divided and each branch is able to check the actions of the other two.

- Congress is divided into an upper and lower house — the Senate and the House of Representatives.

Famous People

Columbus (1451-1506): explorer who sailed to North America and claimed it for Spain

Only a small number of people from the past have become so **famous** that their names are still remembered long after their death. Some of these people became famous for their **daring deeds** and **leadership**. Others are famous for helping to **improve other people's lives**. Many are remembered because the stories of their lives are so **dramatic**. Today, television, motion

pictures, and newspapers can quickly make people famous all over the world. In the past it was difficult to become well known. Here you can find out just a little about some of the most famous people.

Tutankhamun

Tutankhamun was a **pharaoh**, or ruler, of ancient Egypt. He died in 1352 B.C. He has become famous because, more than 3,000 years after his death, his tomb was discovered containing gold, jewels, and many other beautiful objects.

- Tutankhamun became pharaoh when he was 11 years old. He married an Egyptian princess.

- He died when he was about 18.

- In 1922 archaeologists discovered his tomb in Egypt in the Valley of the Kings.

- The pharaoh's body was mummified (preserved and wrapped in bandages) inside a coffin made of solid gold.

Queen Elizabeth I

Queen Elizabeth I lived from 1533 to 1603. She was one of the most famous **rulers of England**. Her court was well known for its poets, painters, musicians, and playwrights.

- Elizabeth was born in 1533, the daughter of King Henry VIII and Anne Boleyn. When Elizabeth was a baby, her father had her mother beheaded.

- When she was a young girl she was locked up for a while in the Tower of London by her half-sister Mary. Mary thought Elizabeth was plotting against her.

- After Mary's death, Elizabeth came to the throne of England. She was 25 and reigned for another 45 years.

Mozart (1756-1791): musical genius who began composing at the age of five

Queen Victoria (1819-1901): popular and longest-reigning British monarch

Picasso (1881-1973): Spanish painter who influenced modern art styles

Napoleon Bonaparte

Napoleon, who lived from 1769 to 1821, was a famous French **leader** and **ruler**. He conquered large parts of Europe and made himself emperor over them.

● He was born on the island of Corsica and went to a military school in Paris.

● He became head of the French army and won many victories throughout Europe.

● He reorganized France by improving the law, banks, trade, and education. He also encouraged the sciences and the arts.

● In 1804 he crowned himself Emperor of France. His wife, Josephine, was made Empress.

● When his enemies in Europe invaded France, Napoleon was sent into exile on Elba, an island off the coast of Italy.

● He escaped from Elba and returned to France, gathering an army. However, he was finally beaten at the Battle of Waterloo.

Abraham Lincoln

Abraham Lincoln lived from 1809 to 1865. From a humble background he rose to become the sixteenth **president of the United States**, leading the country at a dramatic point in its history.

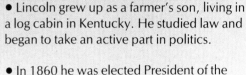
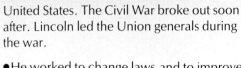

● Lincoln grew up as a farmer's son, living in a log cabin in Kentucky. He studied law and began to take an active part in politics.

● In 1860 he was elected President of the United States. The Civil War broke out soon after. Lincoln led the Union generals during the war.

● He worked to change laws and to improve life for all Americans. In particular he brought about the end of slavery in the United States.

● Toward the end of the Civil War, Lincoln was shot dead by a political enemy while at the theater.

Strange but true

● The Ancient Egyptians used to mummify animals such as cats, baboons, dogs, and crocodiles as well as kings.

● Potatoes and tobacco were unknown in Europe until Sir Walter Raleigh brought them back from North America during the reign of Elizabeth I.

● Abraham Lincoln went to school for less than a year. He taught himself to read and write.

Gandhi

Gandhi was an important **Indian leader**. He lived from 1869 to 1948. During his life he worked to bring peace and justice to the world. His ideas and courage made him admired in many countries.

● He was born in India and went to study law in London when he was 19.

● As a lawyer in South Africa and in India he worked to help the poor and suffering, trying to change laws that were unfair.

● Many Indian people called him "Mahatma," which means "great soul."

● He led the Indian people in their struggle for independence from Britain.

● Gandhi believed there was no need to be violent to solve the world's problems. To draw attention to his beliefs he sometimes went on hunger-strikes that endangered his life.

● Shortly after India became independent, Gandhi was shot dead by an enemy at an open-air prayer meeting.

The Animal Kingdom

Here are some of the smaller animal groups:

Coelenterates — jellyfish, corals, sea anemones

Animals are creatures that breathe in **oxygen**. They have to **eat** plants or other animals in order to survive.

Animals have been on the Earth in one form or another for about 700 million years. The first animals were tiny single-celled creatures.

Single-celled creatures

Today, several million different kinds of animals live on Earth. Scientists divide them into **related groups**.

Animal groups

Here are the main **animal groups**:

- Mammals (see p.74) include such different examples as bats, whales, cats, kangaroos, and humans. Many large creatures belong to this group.

- Reptiles (see p.80) include snakes, lizards, turtles, and crocodiles. Up to 65 million years ago, reptiles dominated the Earth as dinosaurs.

- Amphibians (see p.80) have bodies that are adapted to live on land or in water. This group includes frogs, toads, newts, and salamanders.

Strange but true

- The present day is sometimes called the "Age of the Insects." Insects vastly outnumber all the other animal groups.

- Because grass gives so little nourishment, cows must graze all day to get enough for their needs.

- Some scientists think that apes and humans are descended from a type of rodent, rather like a rat.

Animal food

Animals eat different kinds of **food**, depending on their size, the type of stomach they have, and the food available.

- Animals that eat only plants are called herbivores.

Herbivorous zebra

- Animals that eat both meat and plants are called omnivores.

- Animals that eat only meat are called carnivores.

Carnivorous lion

- Predators help to strengthen the animal population. They tend to catch and kill the weakest members of an animal group. The strongest ones are left alive. These are more likely to breed healthy offspring.

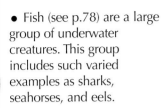

Mollusks —
slugs, snails,
clams, octopuses

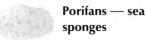

Porifans — sea
sponges

Annelids —
earthworms,
ragworms

Echinoderms —
starfish, sea-
urchins

● Fish (see p.78) are a large group of underwater creatures. This group includes such varied examples as sharks, seahorses, and eels.

● The bird group (see p.82) includes many different flying birds and some non-flying kinds. Examples of this group are found all over the world.

● Insects (see p.76) are by far the largest group of animals in the world today. They include ants, beetles, bees, butterflies, lice, and flies.

● Arachnids have eight legs, in contrast to the six-legged insects. The arachnid group includes scorpions, harvestmen, mites, and spiders.

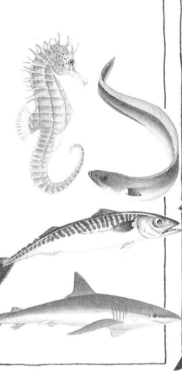

The food chain

Animals are linked together by what they eat, forming a **food chain**. The smallest animals eat plants. They are in turn eaten by larger animals, and so on. Here is a typical food chain:

Plant (eaten by aphid)

Spider (eaten by small bird)

Bird of prey (the end of this chain)

Small bird (eaten by bird of prey)

Aphid (eaten by spider)

Mouse (eaten by bird of prey)

Mammals

Mammals are a very successful group of animals found all over the world. There are about **4,050 species** in all.

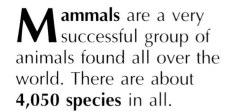

Rodent

Bat

Sea mammal

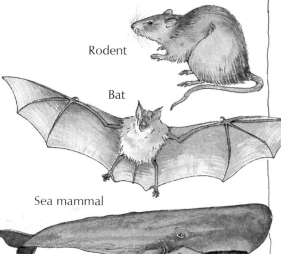

The mammal family includes **bats**, **rodents** (small gnawing creatures such as rats and mice), and some sea animals such as **whales** and **dolphins**. It also includes **primates**. Human beings are part of the primate group, along with lemurs, monkeys, and apes.

Primates

Mammal facts

Mammals have:

● Hairy bodies, to help them keep warm. Some mammals have thick fur; some only have a fine fur.

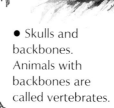

● Skulls and backbones. Animals with backbones are called vertebrates.

● Warm blood, which means that they can keep their own body temperature at a comfortable level.

● The ability to suckle their young, which means that they can feed babies with milk from their body.

Different kinds of mammal

Zoologists split mammals into three **scientific groups**. Each group gives birth to babies in a different way.

● Monotremes lay eggs and hatch their young. There are only two types of monotremes: the duck-billed platypus from Australia and the spiny anteaters or echidnas from Australia and New Guinea.

Duck-billed platypus

● Marsupial mammal babies are born very tiny and undeveloped. Most marsupial babies finish growing inside pouches on their mother's body. Kangaroos are marsupials.

● Placental mammal babies are born alive and well-developed. When a placental baby is growing inside its mother it lives inside a kind of protective sac. Its blood supply is linked to its mother's.

A human embryo

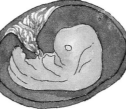

Baby in pouch

Giant panda (China)

Javan rhino (Java)

Mountain gorilla (Congo, Uganda)

Amazing mammals

Mammals are lots of different shapes and sizes. That is partly because they have developed to survive in many different kinds of places. Here are some **mammal record-breakers**:

● The world's noisiest land animals are South American howler monkeys. When the male monkeys call, their screams can be heard from 10 miles (16 km) away.

● The world's largest land mammal is the African elephant. Adult bull elephants grow over 10 feet (3 m) tall and weigh about 6 tons.

● Cheetahs are the world's fastest animals on land. They can run up to 60 mph (100 km/h) over short distances.

● The giraffe is the tallest mammal in the world. It can grow over 16 feet (5 m). It has a long neck so that it can reach leaves high up in the trees.

Primates

Primates are the most well-developed mammals. They have:

● Complex brains, which means that they are able to think better than most other creatures in the animal kingdom.

● The ability to stand upright for long periods.

● More highly-developed hands than any other animal group. They can use their hands for all kinds of complicated skills.

● Eyes set side by side in the front of the head, which means that they can see more clearly than most other creatures.

Strange but true

● Many mammals sleep for long periods. Lions sleep up to 20 hours a day.

● Gorillas sleep in nests which they build in low branches of trees.

● Lions and tigers have been successfully crossed to make a new animal — the "tigon."

● Blue whale babies weigh up to 7 tons (7,000 kg) at birth.

75

Insects

Insects are the biggest animal group. There are vast numbers of them, and there are probably many unknown types of insect still to be discovered.

Insects are found all over the world, even in frozen lands and in scorching deserts where other animals find it hard to survive.

Most insects live on their own for most of their lives, but some insects, such as bees, live in **organized communities** with many companions of the same type.

Insect parts

Insects do not all look the same, but they all have some characteristics in common. **All insects** have:

- A protective outer covering called an "exoskeleton." Insects are "invertebrates," which means that they do not have backbones. They do have internal skeletons.

- A head which carries the eyes, antennae, and feeding parts.

- An abdomen, made up of a series of segments. Vital organs such as the heart are inside.

- A thorax, which carries legs and sometimes wings.

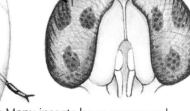

Head

Thorax

Eye

Abdomen

- Three pairs of jointed legs.

- Cold blood, which means that they cannot control their own body temperature. They rely on the temperature of their surroundings to keep them alive.

- Many insects have compound eyes, made of hundreds of tiny lenses.

Strange but true

- Some butterflies have scented wings, to attract a mate.

- Some insects produce tiny lights on their bodies to attract mates.

- Crickets have ears positioned on their knees.

- Prehistoric dragonflies had wingspans up to 30 inches (76 cm) across, wider than many modern birds.

Growing up

Some insects go through a complete change of body and appearance called **metamorphosis**. There are four stages:

1. The female insect lays lots of tiny eggs, sometimes on the underside of a leaf.

2. The eggs hatch into larvae. Caterpillars, grubs, and maggots are all forms of insect larvae.

3. When the larva has grown enough it changes into a pupa (or chrysalis), inside a hard case called a cocoon, the insect's body dissolves and reforms into a new shape.

4. Once the change has occurred, the cocoon splits open and the adult insect comes out. Butterflies, moths, beetles, flies, ants, and bees all go through metamorphosis.

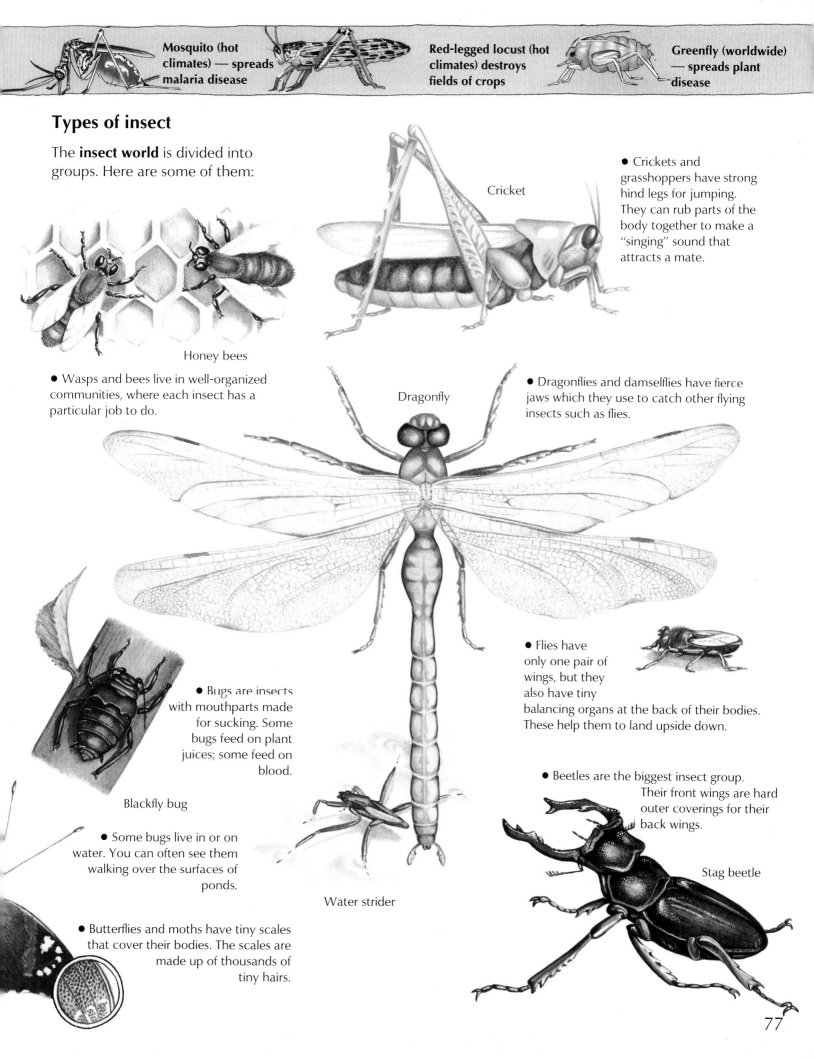

Mosquito (hot climates) — spreads malaria disease

Red-legged locust (hot climates) destroys fields of crops

Greenfly (worldwide) — spreads plant disease

Types of insect

The **insect world** is divided into groups. Here are some of them:

Honey bees

• Wasps and bees live in well-organized communities, where each insect has a particular job to do.

Cricket

• Crickets and grasshoppers have strong hind legs for jumping. They can rub parts of the body together to make a "singing" sound that attracts a mate.

Dragonfly

• Dragonflies and damselflies have fierce jaws which they use to catch other flying insects such as flies.

• Bugs are insects with mouthparts made for sucking. Some bugs feed on plant juices; some feed on blood.

Blackfly bug

• Some bugs live in or on water. You can often see them walking over the surfaces of ponds.

• Butterflies and moths have tiny scales that cover their bodies. The scales are made up of thousands of tiny hairs.

Water strider

• Flies have only one pair of wings, but they also have tiny balancing organs at the back of their bodies. These help them to land upside down.

• Beetles are the biggest insect group. Their front wings are hard outer coverings for their back wings.

Stag beetle

77

Fish

Fish live in oceans, rivers, lakes, and ponds. They are **cold-blooded**, which means that they cannnot change thier own body temperature.

There are about 20,000 different **species**, ranging from giant whale sharks about 40 feet (12 m) long to dwarf gobies no bigger than a thumbnail.

Bony fish

Most fish belong to the **bony fish** group, which means that they have **bone skeletons** inside their bodies. Many of the fish we eat are of this kind.

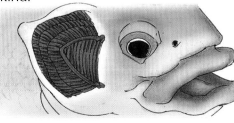

● Bony fish have a gill slit on either side of the body. The slits are covered over with flaps of skin.

● Flat fish, such as flounders, are bony. They lie on one side of their bodies.

Jawless fish

Lampreys and hagfish belong to the **jawless** fish group.

● Jawless fish have round sucking funnels for mouths. They have sharp teeth to hook onto their prey.

● Lampreys suck the blood of prey. Hagfish eat the flesh of their victims.

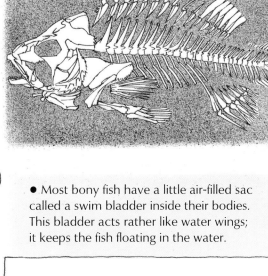

● Most bony fish have a little air-filled sac called a swim bladder inside their bodies. This bladder acts rather like water wings; it keeps the fish floating in the water.

Fish facts

Most fish have:

● Backbones. All fish are vertebrates.

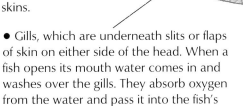

● A scaly skin, which stays moist and waterproof. Eels and lampreys are the only fish to have smooth skins.

● Gills, which are underneath slits or flaps of skin on either side of the head. When a fish opens its mouth water comes in and washes over the gills. They absorb oxygen from the water and pass it into the fish's body. Waste water goes out through the slits.

Strange but true

● Pufferfish can puff their bodies up to scare away enemies.

● Salmon live in the sea, but they return to breed in the river where they were born.

● There are probably about a quintillion herring in the Atlantic Ocean (a million million million).

● A female cod can lay up to 9 million eggs.

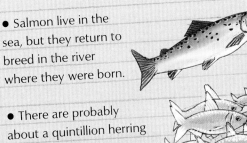

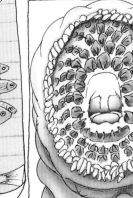

Jawless fish mouth

Lamprey

Fishmeal (used in fertilizers)

Fish oil (used in various products)

Arrow heads and harpoon hooks (fish teeth)

Cartilaginous fish

The **cartilaginous** fish family includes sharks, rays, skate, and dogfish. They have:

● Skeletons made of tough, gristly cartilage instead of bones.

● No swim bladders. This makes them heavier than water. They must keep swimming all the time, or they will sink.

● Fins and a tail that help the fish to steer through the water.

● A streamlined shape, which is smooth and curved. This makes it easier for the fish to slip smoothly through the water.

● Five gill slits on either side of the body. These are easy to see because they are not covered by skin flaps.

● A special sense called a "lateral line," made of groups of cells which form a line along both sides of the body. The cells can feel changes of pressure in the water around them, caused by objects such as rocks and other fish.

Fish reproduction

Most female fish lay thousands of tiny **eggs** that float in the water. Many of the eggs are eaten by predators before they hatch.

● The male seahorse is unusual because it carries the eggs instead of the female. The female lays her eggs into a pouch on the male's body. When the babies hatch they stay in the pouch while they grow.

● Unlike most fish, tilapia look after their young. When its family is threatened this fish opens its mouth and its babies swim inside for safety.

● Skate and dogfish lay their eggs inside horny cases, which are known as mermaids' purses. Sometimes the old discarded cases can be found washed up on the beach.

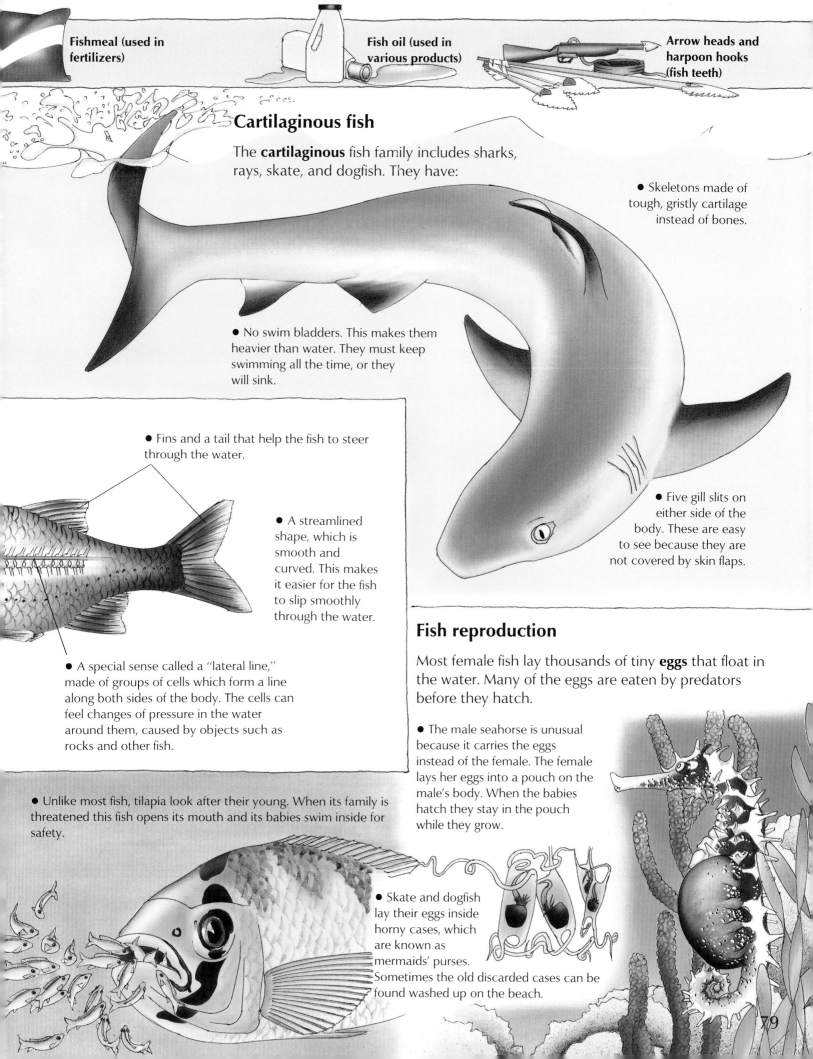

79

Reptiles and Amphibians

Amphibians are a group of animals that spend part of their lives in water and part of their lives on land. **Frogs**, **toads**, **newts**, and **salamanders** are all examples.

Amphibians

Reptiles live and breed mostly on land, although a few live in water. **Snakes**, **lizards**, **crocodiles**, and **turtles** are all reptiles.

Reptiles

Amphibians

Amphibians have moist **slimy skin**. They always live near **fresh water** because they must return there in order to breed.

● There are swimming frogs, burrowing frogs, climbing frogs, and even flying frogs that can glide from tree to tree.

● Like most amphibians, baby frogs metamorphose, which means that they change completely before they become adults (see p.76). They grow from tiny tadpoles into frogs.

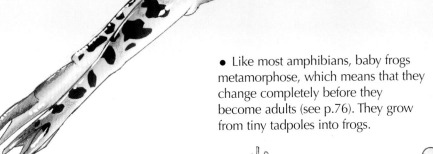

Spawn   Tadpole   Legs form   Frog

Reptiles

Reptiles are **cold-blooded**, which is why they need to live in warm climates. They have scaly, **waterproof skin** and most of them lay **eggs** with tough protective shells.

Lizards are reptiles with scaly bodies and four limbs:

● Some lizards have collars of skin which they puff out to make themselves look bigger when they are excited or scared.

Tortoises, **terrapins**, and **turtles** are reptiles with protective shells.

Frilled lizard

● Turtles live in seawater. They only come ashore to lay their eggs.

● The largest, heaviest lizard is the komodo dragon from Indonesia. It can grow up to 10 feet (3 m) long, and is a fierce hunter.

Komodo dragon

80

Hairy frog
(Central Africa)

Surinam toad
(S. America)

Horned Escuerzo
(S. America)

• Newts and salamanders are long, thin, and lizardlike. There are many different types and colors.

Tiger salamander (N. America)

• There is a third small group of amphibians called caecilians. They are strange creatures that look more like earthworms. They spend their lives burrowing in sand and mud.

Mexican caecilian

Strange but true

• Snakes never close their eyes at any time.

• Chameleon lizards can look in two directions at once.

• If a lizard's tail is broken off, it can usually grow a new one.

• Ancient Egyptians thought crocodiles were sacred. They mummified (preserved) thousands of them.

Snakes are limbless reptiles.

• Some snakes have poisonous fangs. When they bite, poison runs down into the wound through grooves in the fangs.

Poisonous fangs

• The fanged cobra is among the most dangerous snakes in the world. It raises a hood of skin on its neck when it feels threatened.

• Some snakes kill their victims by coiling around them and squeezing them to death. These "constricting" snakes are not poisonous but they are often very large. The anaconda and python are examples.

Cobra

There are 120 species of **crocodiles** and **alligators**.

• The difference between the two is that when a crocodile's mouth is closed you can see its fourth tooth sticking out over the lower jaw.

Crocodiles

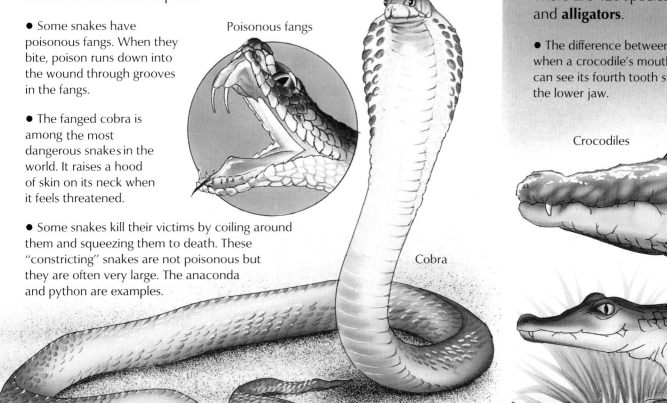
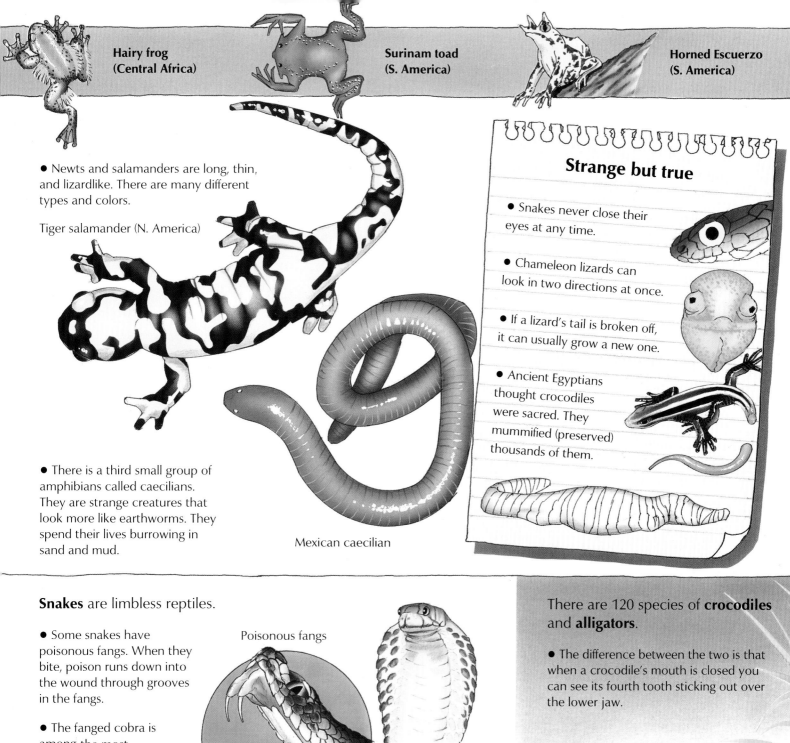

Birds

Birds are **warm-blooded** animals with **internal skeletons**. They all have **wings** and **feathers**, although not all birds can fly. There is a wide variety of birds. They live in many different habitats all over the world, from icy polar lands to hot tropical rain forests. Some birds live alone or in small groups. Others live in **colonies** numbering many thousands.

Bird facts

Most birds have bodies designed for flight. All **flying birds** have these physical features:

● A light, waterproof covering of feathers over most of the body. They help birds to fly and also keep body heat in, so the bird stays warm.

● A streamlined body shape. This helps birds to travel smoothly through the air by cutting down air resistance.

● Two wings covered with extra-strong flight feathers. The wings help to raise the bird into the air and the bird keeps itself aloft by flapping them.

● Scaly legs and feet with three or four toes and sharp claws.

● A horny pointed beak for feeding. Different birds have differently shaped beaks.

● Lightweight, partly hollow internal bones.

Strange but true

● The earliest known bird, called Archaeopteryx, lived 150 million years ago. Unlike modern birds it had teeth.

● Swifts spend almost all their lives in the air. They only land to breed.

● Flamingoes are pink because their bodies take on the pink color of the shrimps they eat.

● The Andean sword-billed hummingbird has a beak longer than its body.

Eggs and nests

Bird species breed at certain times of the year, when the weather is mild and there is a good supply of food.

● Some male birds use complicated dances, special songs, or displays to attract females. For instance, the male peacock shows off its bright tail feathers to interest a mate.

Peacock male

● Eggs vary in color and shape. For instance, some are speckled so that they are difficult to spot when they are lying in a nest.

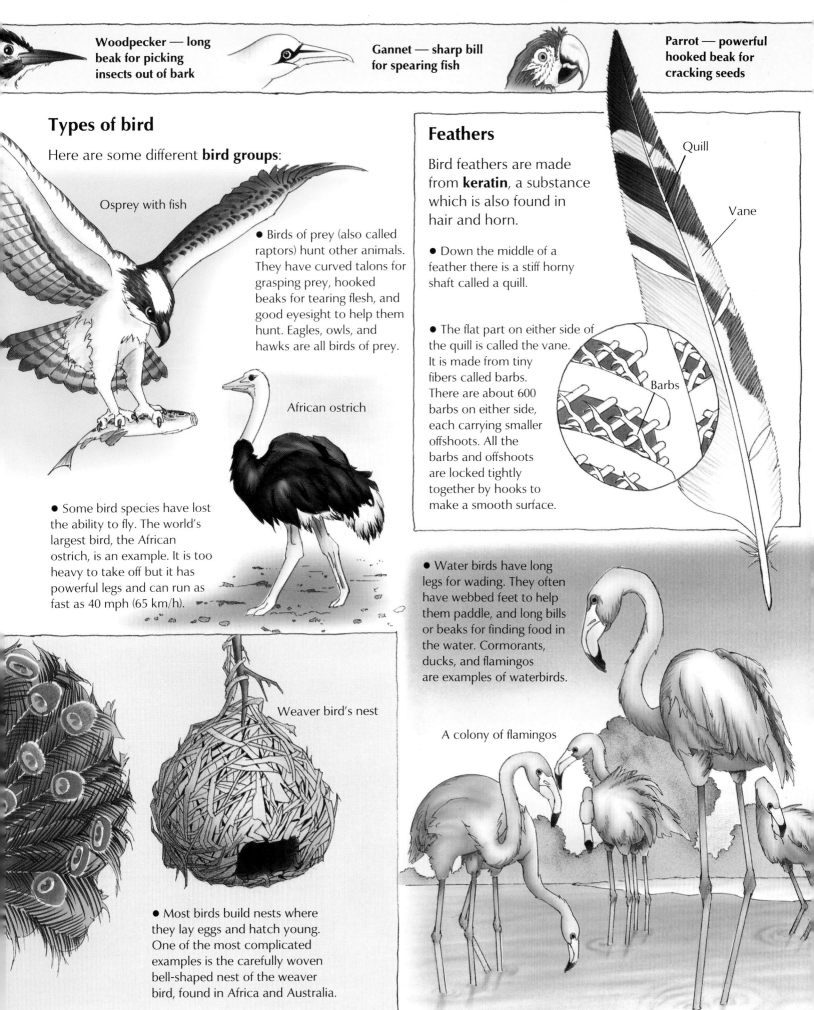

Types of bird

Here are some different **bird groups**:

Osprey with fish

• Birds of prey (also called raptors) hunt other animals. They have curved talons for grasping prey, hooked beaks for tearing flesh, and good eyesight to help them hunt. Eagles, owls, and hawks are all birds of prey.

African ostrich

• Some bird species have lost the ability to fly. The world's largest bird, the African ostrich, is an example. It is too heavy to take off but it has powerful legs and can run as fast as 40 mph (65 km/h).

Weaver bird's nest

• Most birds build nests where they lay eggs and hatch young. One of the most complicated examples is the carefully woven bell-shaped nest of the weaver bird, found in Africa and Australia.

Feathers

Bird feathers are made from **keratin**, a substance which is also found in hair and horn.

• Down the middle of a feather there is a stiff horny shaft called a quill.

• The flat part on either side of the quill is called the vane. It is made from tiny fibers called barbs. There are about 600 barbs on either side, each carrying smaller offshoots. All the barbs and offshoots are locked tightly together by hooks to make a smooth surface.

Quill

Vane

Barbs

• Water birds have long legs for wading. They often have webbed feet to help them paddle, and long bills or beaks for finding food in the water. Cormorants, ducks, and flamingos are examples of waterbirds.

A colony of flamingos

83

Grassland Animals

Grasslands are wide, open areas where grasses and shrubs grow.

Temperate grasslands are found in cool parts of the world in the middle of large land masses, where rainfall is low. These areas are often used for cattle.

Tropical grassland is found mainly in Africa and South America. In Africa it is called **savanna**, and in South America it is called **pampas**. Here rain falls only in summer.

Tropical grassland provides a home for many wild animals.

Plant-eating animals

Most grassland animals are **grazers**, eating grass and other plants. Grazers live together in **herds**, for safety. They move about looking for fresh pastures and water pools. Here are some examples of plant-eaters on the **African savanna**:

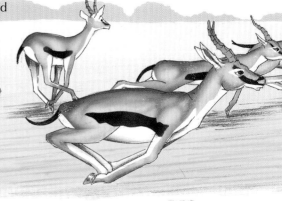

● Antelope live in most tropical grassland areas. Species include orynx, eland, and gazelles. Although they are only 2 feet (60 cm) tall, gazelles can run at 55 mph (90 km/h) to escape danger.

● The African savanna has shrubs and trees as well as grass. These provide food for giraffes, elephants, and rhino.

● Zebras move in large herds, often accompanied by wildebeest. While some zebras graze, others stay on the lookout for lions, their main enemy. Zebras can hear and smell better than most other grazing creatures.

Strange but true

● Elephants spend 23 hours a day eating.

● Some antelope can leap 10 feet (3 m) in the air from a standing start.

● Vultures sometimes eat so much they can't take off again.

● No two zebras have exactly the same pattern of stripes. Like human fingerprints, each zebra pattern is unique.

Zebras prefer taller grasses

Some antelope stand on their hind legs to reach low tree branches

Giraffes and elephants eat the tops of trees

Meat-eaters

The main threat to the grassland plant-eaters are **meat-eaters** such as lions, leopards, and hunting dogs.

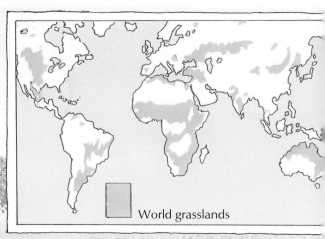
World grasslands

● Lions live in groups called prides. They hunt and kill only when they are hungry. Antelope and zebras are their favorite food.

● African hunting dogs live in large, well-organized packs. They hunt together, separating weak or young animals from herds.

Scavengers

Scavengers are creatures who eat the leftovers from dead animal carcasses. When the grassland hunters have finished with their prey, the scavengers move in to pick the bones clean.

● Vultures are large birds found in many grassland areas of the world. They use their keen eyesight to spot dead animals far below them.

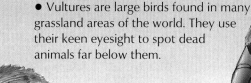

● Hyenas usually eat the remains of another animal's kill, but they will hunt if food is scarce. Their "chuckling" hunting cry sounds rather like a human laugh.

● Although vultures and hyenas have a bad reputation, they provide a useful "garbage disposal" service, because if carcasses are left to rot they attract flies and disease.

Rain Forest Animals

Rain forests are hot, steamy jungles that grow in areas on either side of the equator — an imaginary line that circles the middle of the Earth. Rain forest areas have **high temperatures** and **heavy rainfall** all the year round. They are the richest animal and plant habitats in the world.

Equator

Rain forest area

Strange but true

• The African jungle okapi's tongue is so long, it can be used to lick the creature's eyes.

• The African giant snail grows up to 15 inches (39 cm) long.

• The strongest-known animal poison comes from the arrow-poison frog.

• The Amazon "Jesus Christ lizard" can run across water.

Rain forest birds

Many **birds** make their home in the rain forest trees.

Hornbill

• Each forest region has its own giant eagle species. These birds build huge twig platforms on top of the highest trees.

Toucan

• Brightly-colored macaws, hornbills, and toucans make their nests in holes in tree trunks.

Macaw

• There are lots of different hummingbird species in the Amazon region. They hover by flowers, drinking the sweet nectar with their long beaks.

Hummingbird

Rain forest insects

There are many, many thousands of different insect species in the rain forests.

• Ants can be found everywhere in the rain forests. Huge columns of fierce army ants travel through the forest areas of Central America, destroying everything in their path.

• Giant butterflies flit among the trees. Many of them are brightly-colored. This is a signal that they taste horrible.

Monkey-eating eagle —
Philippines

Golden lion marmoset —
South America

Orangutan —
Sumatra

Gliders

- The Asian flying squirrel glides from tree to tree using the skin stretched between its legs like a parachute.

Flying squirrel

Flying snake

- When the flying snake launches itself, it flattens its body into a broad ribbon shape so that it can glide through the air.

Animals in the trees

Most rain forest **mammals** live up in the tree branches.

- The Amazon sloth hangs motionless and upside down for days on end. It has a shaggy coat and long claws for gripping branches.

Sloth

Margay

- There are lots of different jungle monkeys. Some of them have prehensile tails, which can be used like a hand to grip onto things.

- The Amazon margay and the ocelot are types of rain forest cat. Both are expert tree climbers.

Ocelot

Reptiles

Rain forests make ideal homes for warmth-loving **reptiles**.

- The world's biggest insect, the Goliath beetle, lives in African rain forests.

- The bushmaster snake lives among tree branches. It has heat-sensitive patches on its head, so it can find possible victims by sensing their body heat. Its bite can kill humans.

- The world's heaviest snake is the anaconda, found in South America and Trinidad. It can weigh up to 330 pounds (150 kg), and strangles its prey by coiling around it. It feeds mainly on birds, deer, and rodents.

87

Animal Babies

Pregnancies vary in length. Here are some mammal examples:

Golden hamster: two and a half weeks

All animal species produce **new generations**. Most species reproduce when the climate and food supply is right. For instance, many birds hatch new families in spring, when there is plenty of food to eat.

Within the animal kingdom there are many different kinds of **babies** and methods of **giving birth**.

Strange but true

● Gray tree frogs build nests of foam hanging over water. The tadpoles drop out of the foam when they hatch.

● The ichneumon fly injects its eggs into a caterpillar. The larvae hatch and eat their way out.

● Bacteria divide themselves once every 30 minutes or so.

Babies and parents

Some animals are good **parents**, protecting their babies and teaching them survival skills. However, the majority of creatures give no parental care at all.

● Most fish, amphibians, and reptiles lay their eggs and then abandon them. Female fish lay their eggs in the water. Many cannot recognize their own eggs and they often eat them later.

Baby alligator

● The South American discus fish is a good parent. It makes sure that its newborn babies stay close to it for protection, by producing a tasty skin secretion which the babies eat.

● Crocodiles and alligators are caring parents. The female digs a pit, lays her eggs, and then covers them with vegetation. When the babies hatch they squeal at the mother to dig them out.

Discus fish

● Mammal mothers feed and tend their young. For instance, most monkeys carry their babies with them wherever they go. The babies hold on to the mothers' fur.

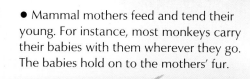

Guinea pig: nine weeks

Human: nine months

Whale: one year

Elephant: two years

• The female midwife toad lays a string of eggs on land. The male then carries the string wrapped around his back legs. When they are ready to hatch he takes the eggs to the water.

Male midwife toad

• Young domestic fowl chicks must teach themselves to feed. They begin by pecking at everything on the ground, including their own toes! Gradually they learn which things are the best to eat.

• Some cuckoos do not look after their own chicks. Instead they lay a single egg in a smaller bird's nest. The cuckoo hatches and pushes the other chicks out. Then it takes all the food the unwitting parent brings.

Cuckoo chick

Ways of reproducing

Here are the four basic ways that animals **reproduce**:

• The simplest form of one-celled animals, such as amoebas, reproduce by splitting themselves in half to form two identical creatures. Animals that behave in this way are called asexual.

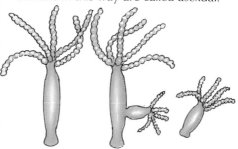

An amoeba splits in two

A hydra buds to make a new hydra

• Some simple animals, such as sea corals and freshwater hydra, produce new creatures by "budding." They grow a new branch which is a small version of the parent. Eventually the branch splits off to become a new individual.

• Most animals have different male and female species. The male produces cells called sperm. The female produces egg cells called ova. The male sperm must join with the female egg before a new animal is produced. This method is called sexual reproduction.

Female egg

Male sperm

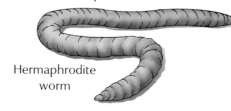

Hermaphrodite worm

• Earthworms and some snails are hermaphrodite. This means that each animal is both male and female, and can produce both sperm and eggs. However, hermaphrodites still have to pair with each other in order to reproduce new creatures.

Eggs and babies

An egg is **fertilized** by a sperm in sexual reproduction. Once this occurs, the egg starts to develop into a new animal.

• Some animals, including most mammals, develop inside their mother's body before they are born. For instance, a newborn foal looks like a miniature version of its parent, and can walk almost immediately.

• Creatures such as birds and many insects lay their eggs once they are fertilized. The babies then develop inside the egg.

Strange Animals

Male tree frog

Some animals have unique **abilities** or **body parts** that no other species possess. These individual features have usually been developed as ways of helping an animal to survive in one way or another. For instance, many creatures have unusual **defense mechanisms** to surprise their enemies.

Some creatures have unique body parts that help them to **feed** or to **survive** in harsh conditions.

Some animals are so extraordinary that scientists are still baffled by the reasons for their behavior.

Amazing animals

Here are some animals with **unusual skills**:

● The tarsier can turn its head right round to look behind it without moving its body.

Tarsier

● When the three-banded armadillo is threatened by enemies, it rolls itself into a very tight armored ball.

Curled-up armadillo

● A gorilla called Koko was taught by humans to use sign language. She used this skill to signal that she wanted a cat as a pet.

Koko the gorilla

● The Texas horned lizard can squirt blood out of its eyes, possibly as a form of defense against enemies.

Strange but true

● Guillemots can "fly" underwater.

● Flies take off backward.

● It takes an elephant calf six months to learn how to use its trunk.

● Crocodiles sometimes climb up trees.

Texas horned lizard

90

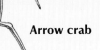
● Most lizards have a tail that can break off if the lizard needs to escape from the grip of a predator. The tail is usually capable of growing again, at least once.

● Giraffes have 18-inch (45-cm) long black tongues which they can use to clean their ears.

Curious connections

Here are some strange animal **similarities**:

● The African elephant's closest relative is the hyrax, which is the size of a rabbit.

● The giraffe has seven neckbones, exactly the same as a human.

Hyrax

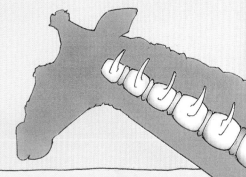

Bizarre birds

Here are some unusual patterns of **bird** behavior:

● Once the female Emperor penguin has laid an egg, the male keeps it warm by balancing it on his feet under a flap of skin.

● Some birds, such as the reed warbler, can sing two tunes at once.

Reed warbler

Hummingbird

● The hummingbird is the only bird that can fly backward.

Fascinating fish

The **underwater world** is full of strange surprises:

● The arawana lives in the flooded Amazon rain forest. It can jump up to 6 feet (2 m) out of the water to feed on small birds or bats in the trees above.

● The African lungfish lives in mud at the bottom of dried-out swamps. It burrows into the ground and covers itself with mucus to keep moist.

●Dolphins, whales, and porpoises talk to each other with clicking and whistling noises.

Endangered Animals

About 5,000 animal species are **endangered**. This means that their numbers are decreasing and that they may die out forever.

An animal species that has disappeared is called **extinct**. The population of some animal species has become so low that they are almost certain to become extinct within the next 20 years.

The endangered panda

Some animals' lives are threatened because their homes and food are being destroyed by **pollution**, **farming**, or **building**. Some are **hunted** for their fur and meat. Sadly, there is a huge illegal trade in "luxury" **animal products** such as rare animal skins and furs.

Land mammals

Although there are organizations to protect endangered wildlife, many animals are still being **poached**, which means that they are killed illegally. Here are some examples:

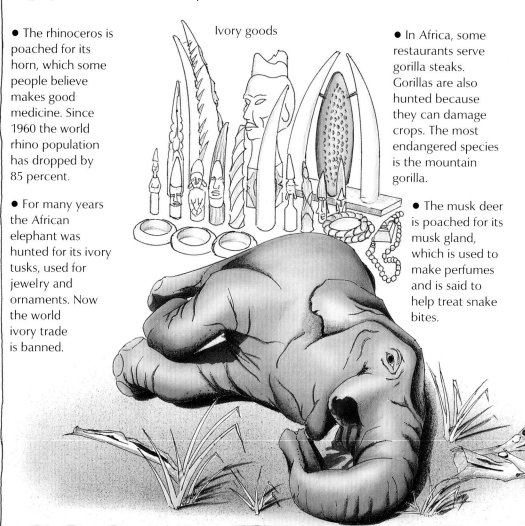

Ivory goods

● The rhinoceros is poached for its horn, which some people believe makes good medicine. Since 1960 the world rhino population has dropped by 85 percent.

● For many years the African elephant was hunted for its ivory tusks, used for jewelry and ornaments. Now the world ivory trade is banned.

● In Africa, some restaurants serve gorilla steaks. Gorillas are also hunted because they can damage crops. The most endangered species is the mountain gorilla.

● The musk deer is poached for its musk gland, which is used to make perfumes and is said to help treat snake bites.

Marine threat

Harmful chemicals and **oil** find their way into the oceans, making them hazardous for ocean life. Some creatures may escape the pollution, only to become victims of other life-threatening dangers:

● Some countries hunt whales for scientific reasons, but sometimes the carcasses are used illegally for food despite strict hunting laws.

● Many dolphins and other sea creatures die when they are trapped in huge fishing nets.

Dolphin

Blue whale

Sea otter
(Pacific coast)

Snow leopard
(Asia)

Lemur
(Madagascar)

Whooping crane
(North America)

Birds in danger

About one fifth of all the world's endangered species are **birds**. **Oil pollution** causes a large number of bird deaths, but many are **trapped** or **shot** by humans. Protection laws are hard to enforce.

Rare hyacinthine macaws

● Exotic birds are often captured illegally and sold worldwide as caged pets. Amongst the rarest species is the large hyacinthine macaw of the Brazilian rain forest.

A cormorant clogged with oil

● An estimated 300,000 seabirds died when oil was spilt from a tanker off Alaska in 1989.

● Several well-known species of fish may eventually disappear because of overfishing. If shoals are caught more quickly than the fish can reproduce, the numbers decline.

● Many turtles have been forced away from the beaches where they breed, as hotels and tourism take over. Sometimes turtles have been deliberately killed.

Loggerhead turtle

Herring shoal

Strange but true

● In Japan you can buy a pair of real turtleshell glasses for about $2,000.

● Rare African gorillas are sometimes shot so that their hands can be used to make ashtrays.

● When a mother river dugong is killed, the tears of her young are bottled and sold as good luck potion.

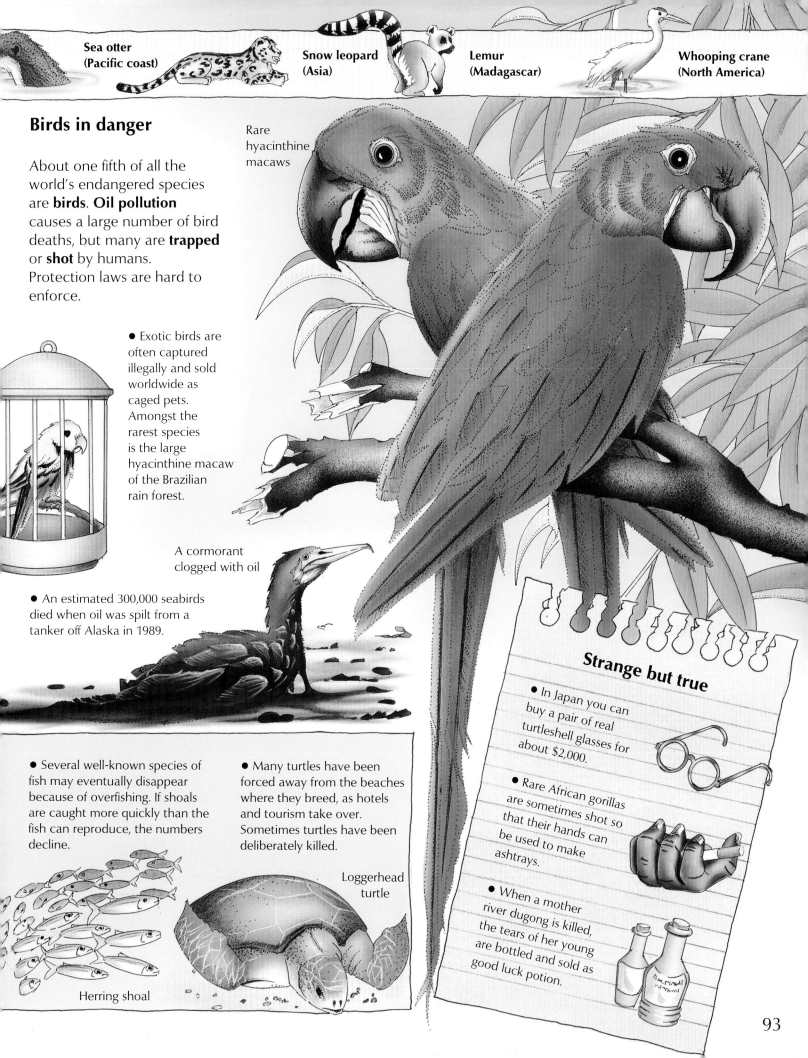

INDEX